MW00633571

TEACHING THE CLASSICS

by Adam and Missy Andrews

Second Edition

Copyright Policy

Teaching the Classics: A Socratic Method for Literary Education
Second Edition, 2017

ISBN 978-0-9983229-1-9

Our duplicating/copying policy for this **Teacher's Manual:**

Home use: The purchaser may copy student-related materials from this Teacher's Manual for use by multiple children within his or her immediate family.

Small group or co-op classes: Each teacher, parent, or student who views the Teaching the Classics DVD seminar must purchase his or her own Teacher's Manual. The purchaser may copy student-related materials from this Teacher's Manual for use in teaching his or her own class. The full Teacher's Manual may not be copied.

Classroom teachers: A Teacher's Manual must be purchased for each teacher or student who views the Teaching the Classics DVD seminar. The purchaser may copy student-related materials from this Teacher's Manual for use in teaching his or her own class. The full Teacher's Manual may not be copied.

Library use: This Teacher's Manual may be checked out of a lending library provided patrons agree not to make copies. Disc media may be checked out as long as patrons are encouraged to purchase their own Teacher's Manuals.

Additional copies of this Teacher's Manual may be purchased from
centerforlit.com/teaching-the-classics or iew.com/ttc-t.

Center For Lit, Inc.
3350 Beck Road
Rice, WA 99167
509.738.2837
adam@centerforlit.com

Institute for Excellence in Writing
8799 N. 387 Road
Locust Grove, OK 74352
800.856.5815
info@iew.com

Printed in the United States of America

CONTENTS

HOW TO USE THIS BOOK

This syllabus is designed as a supplement to the eight-hour DVD seminar *Teaching the Classics*. You should plan to follow along in the syllabus as the DVD sessions unfold, taking notes in the spaces provided.

The DVD seminar will teach you how to study literature with students of all ages. Through discussions of several short stories, it presents the basics of literary analysis in a step-by-step progression. The seminar is normally given over a two-day period, but you may view it over a longer period if you wish.

The seminar is divided into eight one-hour sessions corresponding to the first eight sections of this syllabus. Each session focuses on one area of literary analysis, as summarized in the table of contents above, and features a model discussion of a classic short story. Sessions include live readings of each story, followed by lectures, discussions and practice sessions for teachers. Students in middle school and above may enjoy watching the seminar with their teachers as the sessions are lively and engaging.

After you complete the seminar, you can practice what you have learned with any other piece of literature. The principles of *Teaching the Classics* apply to picture books, historical readers, biographies, classics, poetry, movies and plays – anything, in fact, that tells a story. If you need some suggestions, this syllabus provides graded book lists for students of all ages.

Content of the DVD seminar:

Disc 1: **Tools for Literary Analysis** *(50 minutes)*
Syllabus Section 1

Disc 2: **Style & Context** *(1 hr. 13 minutes)*
Syllabus Section 2

Disc 3: **Setting** *(50 minutes)*
Syllabus Section 3

Disc 4: **Characters** *(52 minutes)*
Syllabus Section 4

Disc 5: **Conflict & Plot** *(52 minutes)*
Syllabus Section 5

Disc 6: **Theme** *(52 minutes)*
Syllabus Section 6

Disc 7: **Practicum** *(48 minutes)*
Syllabus Section 7

Disc 8: **Curriculum & FAQ** *(1 hr. 6 minutes)*
Syllabus Section 8

A Word About Sectarian Content

Teaching the Classics is not a faith-based curriculum. The techniques presented here may be used by any teacher with any work of literature, regardless of religion.

The authors discussed in *Teaching the Classics* include Leo Tolstoy, Rudyard Kipling, Henry Wadsworth Longfellow, Beatrix Potter, and Mark Twain, among others. Like all artists of the Western tradition, these authors addressed religious themes from time to time in their works. The seminar discusses such themes when they appear in the works themselves, in the same way that a sixteenth-century history course might mention the Protestant Reformation. At no time, however, does *Teaching the Classics* assume or advocate any religion.

SECTION 1:
TOOLS FOR LITERARY ANALYSIS

Why Literature?

To experience literature is to see the world through new eyes. As C. S. Lewis stated in his *Experiment in Criticism*, "Those of us who have been true readers all our life seldom fully realise the enormous extension of our being which we owe to authors. . . My own eyes are not enough for me, I will see through those of others." When we read, wc broaden our perspective, so that we are no longer trapped within the limits of our own experience. "In reading great literature," Lewis says, "I become a thousand men and yet remain myself...I see with a myriad eyes, but it is still I who see...I transcend myself; and am never more myself than when I do."

This broadening of perspective is a necessary and crucial part of a strong education. The ability to interact gracefully with important ideas is one mark of a truly educated person, and exposure to such ideas is the only way to become conversant with them! Great literature provides models and examples by which students can hone both their knowledge and expression of the great ideas. Education, however, represents only half of the reason to read.

The other half is that great literature, because it beautifully portrays the tragedy, pathos, and wonder of the human condition, is an end in itself. Literature is not just a textbook of transcendent ideas or a tool for teaching the skill of debate; it is art that richly rewards contemplation. It represents the contributions of its authors to what Mortimer Adler called the Great Conversation about the eternal things. These are the universal ideas that man has contemplated throughout the ages, regardless of his place in space and time. The pleasure and fulfillment that come from reading literature are part of what it is to be human, in the fullest sense. Participation in this conversation sets thinking man apart from the animals.

Why should you want your student to read and understand Shakespeare's *Hamlet*? So that he will get the chance to think critically about literature and about life, of course, but also so that he will have read *Hamlet*. In it he will see and understand, in all its beauty and tragedy and glory, the plight of the human soul. As he reads he will see himself mirrored in Hamlet's nobility and heroism, in his anxiety and indecision, in his glory and his destruction. The student's mind will be uplifted beyond the facts of his own experience to the world of ideas, which will eventually bring to his own life a depth of understanding and a sense of perspective that would otherwise prove unavailable to him.

It is an odd and somewhat disturbing thought, but statistics say that most of us will be utterly forgotten by history within fifty years of our deaths. Achilles, however, still lives, three thousand years later. Hamlet lives. Huckleberry Finn, Augustine of *The Confessions,* Hawthorne's Hester Prynne, Dostoyevsky's Grand Inquisitor – they are all immortal, in a manner of speaking. Why? Because there is something about them, be it the bitterness of Achilles, the repentance of Augustine, the tortured humanity of Hamlet or the earthy wisdom of Huckleberry Finn, that calls out to us at some deep level and makes us answer – that touches us in our humanness, that mirrors our own glorious potential and our own sinful wretchedness. These characters have the power to move and inspire us, to ennoble us.

This is why we study our past, our traditions, our cultural heritage; this is why we read great literature. The world is filled with gifts of beauty, truth, and goodness, and among these gifts are authors, philosophers, and poets. To understand their work is to experience these gifts firsthand.

This seminar is presented with the conviction that even young students can embark on this journey to understand and appreciate literature. They need not wait until they go to college to begin the process; they can start right now. The techniques are easy to learn and easy to teach, and much pleasure and fulfillment awaits him who would apply them.

The following lessons present a model for teaching the skills of literary analysis and interpretation. They are organized according to three important principles, which together form the heart of the *Teaching the Classics* approach to literature:

Principle #1

All works of fiction possess ***common elements***, including Context, Style, and Structure.

Principle #2

Because of their clarity, ***children's stories*** provide the best opportunities for learning these elements.

Principle #3

The best classroom technique for presenting and analyzing literature is the ***Socratic method***.

Principle #1 – The Common Elements of Fiction

Tool: The Story Chart

The key to understanding literature lies in recognizing its structure. All stories are composed of five basic elements: Setting, Characters, Conflict, Plot, and Theme.

The powerful "secret" of literary interpretation is really no secret at all: All stories have these components, even the children's stories you read to your second graders at night! What is more, the elements of fiction are easily perceived in children's literature, even for the children themselves. Children's stories are therefore powerful tools for explaining the elements of fiction to students of all ages. Once grasped, an understanding of these elements may then be applied with great results to the works of the masters.

The lessons in this seminar demonstrate the parts of a story and the techniques used by authors to assemble them into a beautiful whole. The story chart on the next page is a graphic representation of this assembly of components and the relationships that exist between them.

This story chart is the foundational tool of the Teaching the Classics approach to literature. You will be encouraged in the sessions that follow to put each and every story "up on the chart," and through continuous repetition to develop a habit of thinking in these categories. In this way the story chart will become a template for interpretation that you can apply to any work of fiction.

The Story Chart

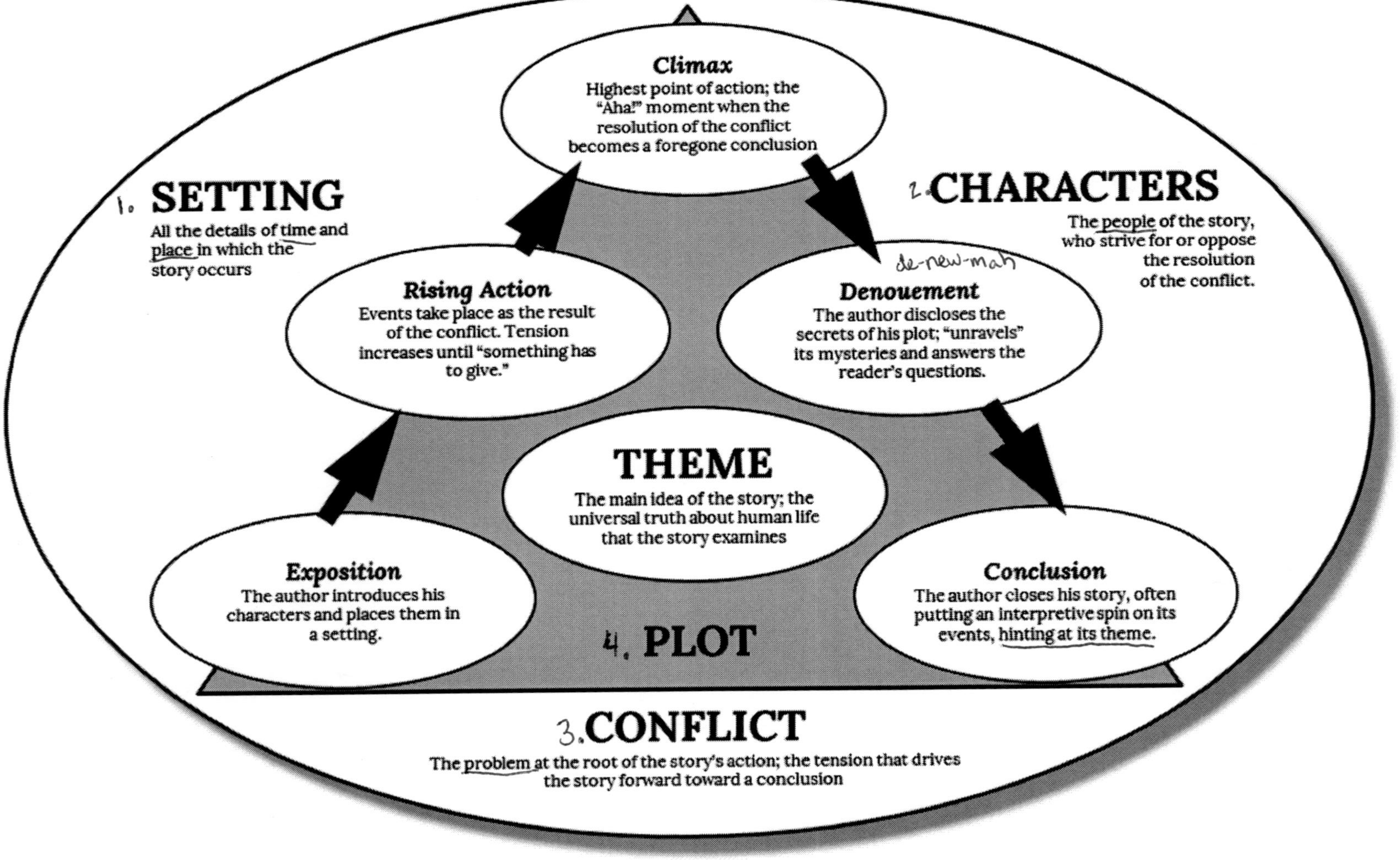

Principle #2 – The Children's Story

Tool: A Children's Story!

Each session in this seminar introduces a separate element of fiction by means of a classic work of children's literature. Discussions of stories by Henry Wadsworth Longfellow, Mark Twain, Rudyard Kipling, Beatrix Potter, Leo Tolstoy and Ernest Lawrence Thayer in the sections that follow will demonstrate the proper techniques for reading and teaching any work of literature.

You may want to use these very stories with your students in the early stages of your own teaching career. Even when you move on to other titles, remember that children's stories provide the best opportunities for learning the fundamentals of literary analysis. Make it a habit to come back to picture books periodically to remind your students (and yourself!) of the basic principles.

Here you can keep a list of children's stories that produce good discussions with your students. For suggestions of other titles to use with *Teaching the Classics*, consult Appendix B of this syllabus.

Principle #3 – The Socratic Method

Tool: The Socratic List

This seminar presents its concepts in the same way that you will be instructed to present them to your own students: by asking questions in the context of a discussion of literature. The pedagogical technique of asking questions is often called the Socratic Method after Socrates, the Greek philosopher who made it famous.

We prefer this method for a variety of reasons:

- First, it is the most immediately effective way to involve the student in the learning process, and avoids dependence on the lecture format, which characterizes most high school and college literature courses. While a good lecture may be informative, a Socratic discussion provides the element of discovery. Students realize information and ideas as they think through well placed questions. In this way, they are best poised to take possession of the ideas themselves.
- Second, use of the Socratic method allows parents and teachers to put instruction in literature in the service of their larger ideological goals. Because the curriculum doesn't claim to tell students what to think about literature, this job is left to the parents – which is as it should be. No matter what your convictions about appropriate reading material, no matter what your idea of the good, the true, and the beautiful, this method will work for you. After learning the techniques of understanding presented here, you will be able to carry on an informed discussion of literature from the standpoint of your own worldview.
- Third, and perhaps most importantly, it allows the teacher to focus on the essential element of education, which is teaching the student how to think. The Socratic method does not begin with answers; it begins with questions. Students are therefore never told what to think before they have a chance to develop their own powers of observation, deduction, and evaluation. In this way, the Socratic method encourages good reading.

The Socratic List (included with this syllabus as Appendix A) provides an easy, step-by-step method for studying literature. It is the means by which you can teach your students to be profound thinkers. Familiarity with these questions gained by long, consistent use will make the understanding of difficult works easy – and this familiarity can be gained *before* the student is able to read those difficult works! Because the elements of fiction are the same for children's stories as for adult stories, the questions used to identify them are the same as well. Young readers may therefore learn real literary analysis at their own reading levels.

It is not necessary to be a college graduate with a literature major or to understand the most technical intricacies of literary interpretation and analysis to participate in Adler's "Great Conversation"; it is only necessary to know which questions to ask – of yourself, and of your students.

Individual questions on the Socratic List are arranged in order of increasing complexity. Generally, the first question for a particular structural element or stylistic device corresponds to the grammar stage of understanding (roughly grades 1 – 6); as such, it will ask for a re-telling of details or a simple description of characteristics. The next questions are aimed at logic level students (grades 7 – 9, for example) and will ask the students to explain the relationship between story elements, draw cause and effect connections between events, and account for significant changes. Finally, rhetoric level questions (aimed at high school students) will demand that the students understand and interact with the worldview of the author, identify and discuss major themes of the work, and evaluate the author's treatment of them.

The Socratic List is designed first of all to stimulate a discussion of literature, which can begin at a very early age. As the student progresses as a writer – especially if he is learning to write well – such discussions can be extended into short, expository essays about particular aspects of a story, either structural or stylistic.

Above all, the Socratic List is designed to stimulate thinking about literature so that students can understand the author. Teachers should be careful not to require the student to evaluate a story before he has experienced it. Grammar and logic before rhetoric, please!

- I claim to know nothing & am only a seeker of truth. Fellow learners.

SECTION 2: STYLE AND CONTEXT

Literary Context

Of primary importance in the study of literature is the context in which it was written. Every story is written by an individual living in a particular culture and period. Consequently, each author's work is, in a sense, a relic of the period in which it was written. Just as George Washington was a product of his time, so also *Pride and Prejudice* is a product of its era. It is impossible that an author may write from any experience other than his own, no matter how fictional the account he weaves might be. He writes folk, fable, truth, and fiction from his own sensory experience. He tells of sunsets he has seen, trips to lands he has traveled, and conversations he has enjoyed. He may use these sensory experiences to create fantasy worlds, languages, and places beyond his reach, but they still smack of the human reality he has experienced.

A passing knowledge of the history of the time in which a piece was penned is therefore invaluable in its study. Social and class structures, moral sensibilities, roles of men and women, theological and philosophical trends and more are at the root of many a tale as authors use their literary genre to examine, criticize, or reflect on the life issues of their time and place. While Jane Austen, for example, ridiculed the rigid social and class structures of her day, Mary Shelley criticized the subjection of women. While Wordsworth, Coleridge and their fellow Romantics contemplated the new, revolutionary spirit of the age, the Victorians who followed concerned themselves with the origins of man, the existence of God, the Scientific Revolution, and problems of urbanization.

In addition to understanding the historical period behind a piece of literature, a good reader must also acknowledge the personal history of the author. While fiction is not autobiography, knowledge of the character and life of the author can at times provide a window into his work. When Mark Twain wrote *The Adventures of Huckleberry Finn*, for example, he not only wrote during a period of racial tension and incongruity in America at large, but also from a wealth of personal experience in the culture of the Mississippi Valley.

"But don't I need a degree in Literature or History to understand these intricacies?"

Of course not! A variety of college level survey texts include short essays on the periods of English literature and on the lives of great authors, many of which are perfect for the home school teacher looking to "bone up" on some history. We recommend especially the Norton Anthology series, which contains dozens of such essays; it is an indispensable source of background information for virtually every classic. Such study guides as *CliffsNotes*, "SparkNotes," or *Masterplots* are also helpful in this regard.

To understand the wide range of personal histories that make authors who they are, consider the following examples:

- **John Milton** (author of *Paradise Lost*) lived in England from 1608 to 1674. He was a Puritan and an outspoken follower of Oliver Cromwell, who ruled England for a time after the execution of Charles I. Milton, in fact, held a prominent position in Cromwell's Protectorate, a fact which nearly cost him his head when Charles II regained the throne. While in his forties, Milton became completely blind, and it is said that he dictated much of his poetry to one of his daughters. The theological and political earmarks of Milton's Puritanism thoroughly characterize his epic poem *Paradise Lost*, while he deals directly with the psychological and spiritual effects of his blindness in several of his greatest poems.

- **Daniel Defoe** (author of *Robinson Crusoe*) lived in England from 1660 to 1731. He was a dissenter from the Church of England, and once mocked the highhanded ways of his Anglican opponents by arguing in a satirical pamphlet that all Dissenters ought to be exterminated. This stunt earned him an arrest and a term in the pillory, where it is said that he castigated his accusers aloud by reading his own satirical poems, while audiences (who had been sold copies) drank his health in the streets. Worth noting is that Defoe's most famous character, Robinson Crusoe, comes to espouse a form of Christianity that would have made him as convinced a Dissenter as Defoe himself.

- **James Fenimore Cooper** (author of *Last of the Mohicans*) lived from 1789 to 1851, and was the first great American novelist. As a young man, he was expelled from Yale, and spent time at sea as a midshipman. Cooper wrote more than fifty books, creating in the process the archetypes of the rugged frontier woodsman and the noble savage.

- **Charles Dickens** (author of *Great Expectations*) lived in England from 1812 to 1870. His father was plagued by debt, and his whole family spent time in debtor's prison in 1824. During this time, the young Dickens worked in a blacking factory, experiencing firsthand the poor work conditions and the sad plight of children before the advent of labor laws. His concern for children remains a prominent characteristic of many of his best novels. Originally writing for magazines (where he was paid by the word!), Dickens eventually became a famous author and public personality. He campaigned against social ills (such as those endured by debtors and other unfortunates) during long lecture tours in Europe and the United States. He is considered by many to be the greatest Victorian novelist.

- **Robert Louis Stevenson** (author of *Treasure Island, Kidnapped,* and *The Black Arrow*) was a Scotsman who lived from 1850 to 1894. He suffered from tuberculosis from childhood. Stevenson traveled extensively, once taking a tour of France and Belgium by canoe. He lived in California for a time in the late 1870s and finally settled in Samoa, where he died. The exotic destinations he visited became the setting of his greatest adventure stories.

- **Harper Lee** (author of *To Kill a Mockingbird*) is an American writer who won the Pulitzer Prize in 1961. Like Scout Finch, Mockingbird's young heroine, Lee is the daughter of a country lawyer and a descendant of Confederate General Robert E. Lee. She grew up in a tiny Alabama town that was no stranger to the tensions and incongruities that characterized the American South generally in the first half of the twentieth century, which tensions also provide conflict in her novel.

Literary Style

The works of revered painters reveal various trends and modes of expression. The Impressionists used techniques such as dabbing and muting colors which up close look like little more than recurrent brush strokes, but afar render beautiful landscapes and portraits. Pointillists refined this style using an arrangement of tiny dots to create their scenes. In contrast to these, artists like John Singer Sargent, though a master of impressionist style, utilized entirely different techniques to create renowned realistic portraits. Picasso and later Modernists broke this mold, distorting realism in accordance with twentieth-century intellectual trends. The artistic principles of Picasso would be unintelligible were they expressed in Sargent's form. One who would understand and appreciate the works of these artists must familiarize himself with the techniques and sentiments attached to them.

Similarly, authors of prose and poetry bring different modes or means of expression – called genres – to their art form. The ideas an author seeks to communicate influence his choice of genre. For example, Dante's *Divine Comedy* utilizes both epic poetic style and satire. A simple satire (or parody) would do violence to the divine nature of Dante's subject matter, while a less satirical rendering of the material would weaken the effects of his social and political commentary, reducing the poem to a collection of tedious rants, *ad hominem* attacks, and the expression of gross personal bitterness. A seasoned author chooses his art form to suit his theme.

Once he makes his choice, the author has at his disposal a full tool box of literary devices available to him to aid his efforts to create atmosphere, mood, character, and plot. Wielded well, these tools may effectively heighten tension, develop atmosphere, deepen the intensity of meaning, and enrich character development within the piece. By using foreshadowing, for example, an author may plant clues to coming joy or disaster, plot twists or despair, suggesting and baiting the reader to consider possible outcomes. With imagery, he may enrich the setting, painting word pictures that evoke feeling and mood. With deft use of an allusion, metaphor, or simile, he may draw on the reader's experience and knowledge to deepen his understanding of characters or themes.

Recognition of some basic literary devices aids a reader in understanding a piece of literature. These devices are road signs to the experienced eye. Find them, and find clues to the author's intention. In addition, an understanding of these tools and their proper usage will enhance the reader's appreciation of the author's artistic ability. It is a talented pen that weaves these expressions into a text with subtlety and finesse.

Stylistic devices are tools used by all authors, not just the Dantes and Shakespeares of the world. Just as John Donne uses metaphor to communicate his sentiments in verse, so Patricia MacLachlan relies upon it in her *All the Places to Love*, as does Jane Yolen in her *Owl Moon.* Metaphors and similes abound in Shakespearean verse, yet are just as abundant within the pages of Ruth Tiller's *Cinnamon, Mint and Mothballs: A Trip to Grandma's House* or Sharon Creech's *Fishing in the Air*. Children's literature and juvenile fiction are replete with expressions of these literary tools. One reading of Henry Wadsworth Longfellow's "Paul Revere's Ride," for example, will expose young readers to devices such as alliteration, assonance, consonance, simile, metaphor, imagery, hyperbole, symbolism, foreshadowing, and onomatopoeia.

Paul Revere's Ride

By Henry Wadsworth Longfellow

Listen my children and you shall hear
Of the midnight ride of Paul Revere,
On the eighteenth of April, in Seventy-five;
Hardly a man is now alive
Who remembers that famous day and year.

He said to his friend, "If the British march
By land or sea from the town to-night,
Hang a lantern aloft in the belfry arch
Of the North Church tower as a signal light
One if by land, and two if by sea;
And I on the opposite shore will be,
Ready to ride and spread the alarm
Through every Middlesex village and farm,
For the country folk to be up and to arm."

Then he said "Good-night!" and with muffled oar
Silently rowed to the Charlestown shore,
Just as the moon rose over the bay,
Where swinging wide at her moorings lay
The Somerset, British man-of-war;
A phantom ship, with each mast and spar
Across the moon like a prison bar,
And a huge black hulk, that was magnified
By its own reflection in the tide.

Meanwhile, his friend, through alley and street,
Wanders and watches with eager ears,
Till in the silence around him he hears
The muster of men at the barrack door,
The sound of arms, and the tramp of feet,
And the measured tread of the grenadiers,
Marching down to their boats on the shore.

Then he climbed the tower of the Old North Church,
By the wooden stairs, with stealthy tread,
To the belfry chamber overhead,
And startled the pigeons from their perch
On the sombre rafters, that round him made
Masses and moving shapes of shade, --
By the trembling ladder, steep and tall,
To the highest window in the wall,
Where he paused to listen and look down
A moment on the roofs of the town
And the moonlight flowing over all.

Beneath, in the churchyard, lay the dead,
In their night encampment on the hill,
Wrapped in silence so deep and still
That he could hear, like a sentinel's tread,
The watchful night-wind, as it went
Creeping along from tent to tent,
And seeming to whisper, "All is well!"
A moment only he feels the spell
Of the place and the hour, and the secret dread
Of the lonely belfry and the dead;

For suddenly all his thoughts are bent
On a shadowy something far away,
Where the river widens to meet the bay,--
A line of black that bends and floats
On the rising tide like a bridge of boats.
Meanwhile, impatient to mount and ride,
Booted and spurred, with a heavy stride
On the opposite shore walked Paul Revere.
Now he patted his horse's side,
Now he gazed at the landscape far and near,

Then, impetuous, stamped the earth,
And turned and tightened his saddle girth;
But mostly he watched with eager search
The belfry tower of the Old North Church,
As it rose above the graves on the hill,
Lonely and spectral and sombre and still.

And lo! as he looks, on the belfry's height
A glimmer, and then a gleam of light!
He springs to the saddle, the bridle he turns,
But lingers and gazes, till full on his sight
A second lamp in the belfry burns!

A hurry of hoofs in a village street,
A shape in the moonlight, a bulk in the dark,
And beneath, from the pebbles, in passing, a spark
Struck out by a steed flying fearless and fleet:
That was all! And yet, through the gloom and the light,
The fate of a nation was riding that night;
And the spark struck out by that steed, in his flight,
Kindled the land into flame with its heat.

He has left the village and mounted the steep,
And beneath him, tranquil and broad and deep,
Is the Mystic, meeting the ocean tides;
And under the alders that skirt its edge,
Now soft on the sand, now loud on the ledge,
Is heard the tramp of his steed as he rides.

It was twelve by the village clock,
When he crossed the bridge into Medford town.
He heard the crowing of the cock,
And the barking of the farmer's dog,
And felt the damp of the river fog
That rises after the sun goes down.

It was one by the village clock,
When he galloped into Lexington.
He saw the gilded weathercock
Swim in the moonlight as he passed,
And the meeting house windows, black and bare,
Gaze at him with a spectral glare,
As if they already stood aghast
At the bloody work they would look upon.

It was two by the village clock,
When he came to the bridge in Concord town.
He heard the bleating of the flock,
And the twitter of birds among the trees,
And felt the breath of the morning breeze
Blowing over the meadow brown.

And one was safe and asleep in his bed
Who at the bridge would be first to fall,
Who that day would be lying dead,
Pierced by a British musket ball.

You know the rest. In the books you have read
How the British Regulars fired and fled, ---
How the farmers gave them ball for ball,
From behind each fence and farmyard wall,
Chasing the redcoats down the lane,
Then crossing the fields to emerge again
Under the trees at the turn of the road,
And only pausing to fire and load.

So through the night rode Paul Revere;
And so through the night went his cry of alarm
To every Middlesex village and farm, ---
A cry of defiance and not of fear,
A voice in the darkness, a knock at the door,
And a word that shall echo forevermore!
For, borne on the night-wind of the Past,
Through all our history, to the last,
In the hour of darkness and peril and need,
The people will waken and listen to hear
The hurrying hoof-beats of that steed,
And the midnight message of Paul Revere.

"Paul Revere's Ride" by H. W. Longfellow

Discussion Notes on Literary Style

Question numbers in parentheses refer to the Socratic List, included in this syllabus as Appendix A.

Does the author use the sounds of our language to create interest in his story? (Question 14)

Onomatopoeia –

Does the author use sound words to tell his story? (Question 14a.)

-stamped
-tramp
-crowing

Assonance –

Does the author use words in sequence or in close proximity which have the same internal vowel sounds? (Question 14c.)

-wanders & watches
-eager ears

↳ creates musical quality & rhythm
↳ mood & atmosphere
↳ attention

Alliteration –

Does the author use words in sequence or in close proximity that repeat the same initial consonant sound? (Question 14e.)

-

Does the author use descriptions and comparisons to create pictures in the reader's mind? (Question 16)

Imagery - ↗word picture

Does the author create snapshots of images in the mind of the reader for the sake of enhancing meaning, creating setting or mood, or developing character? Does he show things to the reader rather than simply telling him about them? (Question 16a.)

Personification –

Does the author represent inanimate objects as being lifelike or human? (Question 16e.)

Simile –

Does the author use the words "like" or "as" in making comparisons between two or more things? (Question 16d.)

Metaphor –

Does the author make comparisons of objects or things without the use of the words "like" or "as"? (Question 16h.)

Does the author use the characters and events in his story to communicate a theme that goes beyond them in some way? (Question 17)

Allusion –

Does the author refer to other works of literature, historical events, works of art, or well-known ideas in his work? (Question 17f.)

Symbolism –

Does the author use any objects, persons, pictures, or things to represent an idea, a virtue or a philosophy in the story? For example, darkness may be used to represent wickedness. Light may be used to represent truth and goodness. A mockingbird may represent innocence. (Question 17i.)

Who is the author? (Question 18)

Was the author associated with a particular social cause or movement? (Examples include temperance, abolitionism, women's suffrage, civil rights, Puritanism, etc.) (Question 21c.)

What events took place in the world during the author's lifetime? Did the author know about them? Was he involved in them? (Question 20b.)

- Famous American Poet
- 1807-1882 - New England
- Jan 1861 - Paul Revere's Ride Published
  - ↳ Abraham Lincoln just elected
  - ↳ 7 of 11 states had already succeeded from Union
- Civil War about to break out

SECTION 3: SETTING

The setting of a story includes all the details of time and place in which the story occurs. Understanding setting and how it relates to the other elements of fiction enables the reader to enter the world of the story quickly and experience it firsthand, as the author intended.

As the following diagram illustrates, setting stands behind the story's plot and themes to provide a spatial and temporal frame of reference that can drive home the author's message with subtle power. The setting of Harper Lee's *To Kill a Mockingbird,* for example – a changing South seething with racial tensions and coming to a kind of maturity – mirrors the changes taking place in the main character and enables the author to stress themes like Lost Innocence and Coming of Age.

Stylistic devices (such as those appearing in "Paul Revere's Ride") are particularly important for establishing the time, place, and mood of a story, and the more we understand their role, the more keenly we will observe their use in the story.

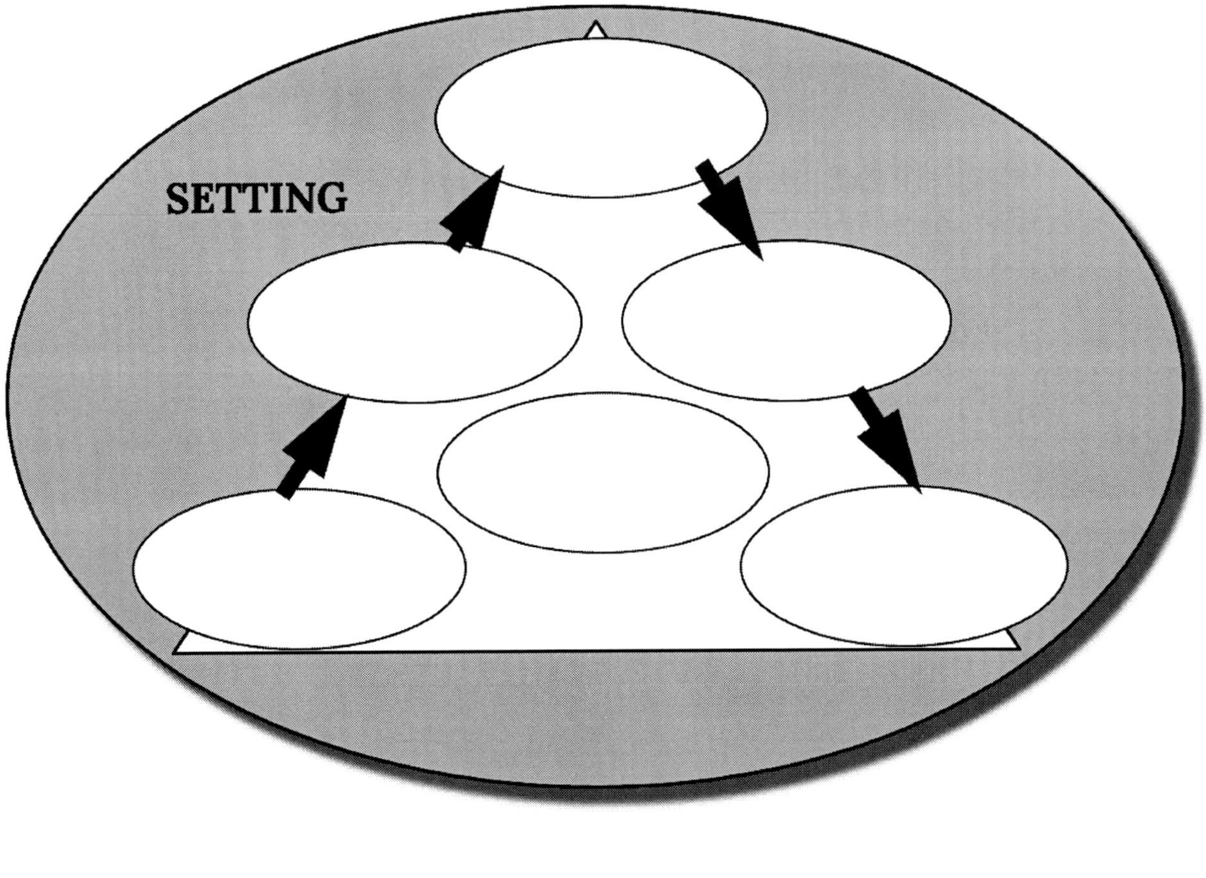

"Rikki-Tikki-Tavi" by Rudyard Kipling

Adapted by Adam Andrews

This is the story of the great war that Rikki-Tikki-Tavi fought single-handed, through the bathrooms and gardens of the big bungalow in Segowlee province in far off India when Victoria ruled.

Teddy and his Mother and Father, who had just come from England, found Rikki-Tikki wandering through the rooms of the big house when they moved in.

Rikki was a mongoose, rather like a little cat in his fur and his tail, but quite like a weasel in his head and his habits. His eyes and the end of his restless nose were pink. He could fluff up his tail till it looked like a bottle brush, and his war cry as he scuttled through the long grass was: "Rikk-tikk-Tikki-Tikki-tchk!"

Rikki's cry frightened Teddy and his mother at first, but Teddy's father reassured them.

"A mongoose will kill snakes," he said. "Teddy's safer with that little beast than if he had a bloodhound to watch him."

And so, Rikki was allowed to stay in the big bungalow with Teddy's family, and he slept on Teddy's bed, tucked snugly under Teddy's chin.

One day Rikki-Tikki went out into the garden to see what was to be seen. It was a large garden, with bushes as big as summer-houses, clumps of bamboos, and thickets of high grass. Rikki-Tikki licked his lips. "This is a splendid hunting-ground," he said, and his tail grew bottle-brushy at the thought of it, and he scuttled up and down the garden, snuffing here and there, till he heard very sorrowful voices in a thorn-bush.

It was Darzee the Tailorbird and his wife, and they were crying piteously.

"What is the matter?" asked Rikki-Tikki.

"We are very miserable," said Darzee. "One of our babies fell out of the nest yesterday and Nag ate him."

"That is very sad," said Rikki, "but I am a stranger here. Who is Nag?"

Darzee and his wife only cowered down in their nest without answering, for from the thick grass there came a low hiss--a horrid cold sound that made Rikki-Tikki jump back two clear feet. Then inch by inch out of the grass rose up the head and spread hood of Nag, the big black cobra, and he was five feet long from tongue to tail. When he had lifted one-third of himself clear of the ground, he stayed balancing to and fro exactly as a dandelion tuft balances in the wind, and he looked at Rikki-Tikki with the wicked snake's eyes that never change their expression.

"Who is Nag?" said he. "I am Nag. Look, and be afraid!"

Now, Rikki-Tikki had never met a live cobra before, but his mother had fed him on dead ones, and he knew that all a grown mongoose's business in life was to fight and eat snakes. Nag knew that too and, at the bottom of his cold heart, he was afraid.

"Well," said Rikki-Tikki, and his tail began to grow bottle-brushy, "do you think it is right for you to eat fledglings out of a nest?"

Nag knew that mongooses in the garden meant death sooner or later for him and his family, and he wanted to get Rikki-Tikki off his guard. So he dropped his head a little, and put it on one side.

"Let us talk," he said. "You eat eggs. Why should not I eat birds?"

"Behind you! Look behind you!" sang Darzee.

Rikki-Tikki knew better than to waste time in staring. He jumped up in the air as high as he could go, and just under him whizzed by the head of Nagaina, Nag's wicked wife. He heard her savage hiss as the stroke missed.

Rikki-Tikki felt his eyes growing red and hot (when a mongoose's eyes grow red, he is angry), and he sat back on his tail and hind legs like a little kangaroo, and looked all round him, and chattered with rage. But Nag and Nagaina had disappeared into the grass.

When the mongoose fights the snake, the victory is only a matter of quickness of eye and quickness of foot--snake's blow against mongoose's jump. Rikki thought about the quickness of Nagaina's blow all that day and into the night.

When the sun had set, Rikki stole off to Teddy's bath-room in search of Nag and Nagaina. At the bottom of the smooth plaster wall there was a brick pulled out to make a sluice for the bath water, and as Rikki-Tikki stole in by the wall, he heard Nag and Nagaina whispering outside in the moonlight.

"When there were no people in the bungalow," said Nagaina to her husband, "did we have any mongoose in the garden? So long as the bungalow is empty, we are king and queen of the garden; and remember that as soon as our eggs in the melon bed hatch (as they may tomorrow), our children will need room and quiet."

"I will go inside tonight," said Nag. "I will kill the big man and his wife and child, and come away quietly. Then the bungalow will be empty, and Rikki-Tikki will go."

Rikki-Tikki tingled all over with rage and hatred at this, and then Nag's head came through the sluice, and his five feet of cold body followed it. Angry as he was, Rikki-Tikki was frightened as he saw the size of the big cobra. Nag coiled himself up, raised his head, and looked into the bathroom in the dark, and Rikki could see his eyes glitter.

"I shall wait here," said Nag. "I shall wait here in the cool till daytime, till the big man comes to take a bath." Nag coiled himself down, coil by coil, round the bulge at the bottom of the water jar, and Rikki-Tikki stayed still as death. Nag fell asleep, and Rikki-Tikki looked at his big back, wondering which would be the best place for a good hold.

"It must be the head," he thought at last; "the head above the hood. And, when I am once there, I must not let go."

Then he jumped. As his teeth sank into Nag's head, Rikki was battered to and fro as a rat is shaken by a dog, but his eyes were red and he held on as the big body cart-whipped over the floor. As he held he closed his jaws tighter and tighter, for he was sure he would be banged to death, and, for the honor of his family, he preferred to be found with his teeth locked. He felt shaken to pieces when, all of a sudden, something went off like a thunderclap just behind him. The big man had been wakened by the noise, and had fired both barrels of a shotgun into Nag just behind the hood.

Rikki-Tikki held on with his eyes shut, for now he was quite sure he was dead. But the big man picked him up and said, "It's the mongoose, Alice. The little chap has saved our lives!"

When morning came, the news of Nag's death was all over the garden. "Now I have Nagaina to settle with," Rikki said to himself, "and there's no knowing when the eggs she spoke of will hatch. Goodness! I must hurry!"

"Where is Nagaina?" panted Rikki to Darzee the Tailorbird, when he got to the garden.

"On the rubbish heap by the stables, mourning for Nag," answered Darzee. "Nag is dead! Great is Rikki-Tikki with the white teeth. Let us sing about the great, the red-eyed Rikki-Tikki!" And Darzee filled his throat and sang. But Rikki was in too great a hurry to stop and listen. He raced for the end of the melon patch near the wall. There in the warm sun he found twenty-five cobra eggs.

"I was not a day too soon," he said, for he could see the baby cobras curled up inside the skins, ready to hatch and kill man or mongoose. He bit off the tops of the eggs as fast as he could, and began to kill the young cobras. At last there was only one egg left, and Rikki-Tikki began to chuckle to himself, when he heard Darzee's wife screaming:

"Rikki-Tikki, Nagaina has gone into the house, and--oh, come quickly--she means killing!"

Rikki-Tikki tumbled backward down the melon-bed with the egg in his mouth, and scuttled to the veranda as hard as he could put foot to the ground. Teddy and his mother and father were there at early breakfast, but Rikki-Tikki saw that they were not eating anything. They sat stone-still, and their faces were white. Nagaina was coiled up on the matting by Teddy's chair, within easy striking distance of Teddy's bare leg, and she was swaying to and fro, singing a song of triumph.

"Son of the big man that killed Nag," she hissed, "stay still. I am not ready yet. Keep very still, all you three! If you move I strike, and if you do not move I strike. Oh, foolish people, who killed my Nag!"

Teddy's eyes were fixed on his father, and all his father could do was to whisper, "Sit still, Teddy. You mustn't move. Teddy, keep still."

Then Rikki-Tikki came up and cried, "Turn round, Nagaina. Turn and fight!"

"All in good time," said she, without moving her eyes. "I will settle my account with you presently. Look at your friends, Rikki-Tikki. They are still and white. They dare not move, and if you come a step nearer I strike."

"Look at your eggs," said Rikki-Tikki, "in the melon bed near the wall. Go and look, Nagaina!"

The big snake turned half around, and saw the egg on the veranda. "Ah-h! Give it to me," she said.

Rikki-Tikki put his paws one on each side of the egg, and his eyes were blood-red. "What price for a snake's egg? For a young cobra? For the last--the very last of the brood? The ants are eating all the others down by the melon bed."

Nagaina spun clear round, forgetting everything for the sake of the one egg. Rikki-Tikki saw Teddy's father shoot out a big hand, catch Teddy by the shoulder, and drag him across the little table with the tea-cups, safe and out of reach of Nagaina.

"Tricked! Tricked! Rikk-tck-tck-tck-tck!" chuckled Rikki-Tikki. "The boy is safe! Come then, Nagaina. Come and fight with me. You shall not be a widow long. Fight!"

Rikki-Tikki was bounding all round Nagaina, keeping just out of reach of her stroke, his little eyes like hot coals. Nagaina gathered herself together and flung out at him. Again and again and again she struck, and each time her head came with a whack on the matting of the veranda and she gathered herself together like a watch spring. Rikki-Tikki danced in a circle to get behind her, and Nagaina spun round, so that the rustle of her tail on the matting sounded like dry leaves blown along by the wind.

Rikki-Tikki had forgotten the egg. At last, while he was drawing breath, Nagaina caught it in her mouth, turned and flew like an arrow down the path, with Rikki-Tikki behind her.

Rikki-Tikki knew that he must catch her, or all the trouble would begin again. She headed straight for the long grass, and as she plunged into the rat-hole where she and Nag used to live, he lunged and clenched his little white teeth on her tail, and went down the hole with her.

Very few mongooses, however wise they may be, care to follow a cobra into its hole. The grass by the mouth of the hole stopped waving, and Darzee said, "It is all over with Rikki-Tikki! We must sing his death song. Valiant Rikki-Tikki is dead! For Nagaina will surely kill him underground."

So Darzee began to sing a very mournful song, but just as he got to the most touching part, the grass quivered again, and Rikki-Tikki, covered with dirt, dragged himself out of the hole leg by leg, licking his whiskers!

Rikki-Tikki shook some of the dust out of his fur and sneezed. "It is all over," he said. "The widow will never come out again."

Rikki-Tikki curled himself up in the grass and slept where he was--slept and slept till it was late in the afternoon, for he had done a hard day's work.

When he returned to the house, Teddy and Teddy's mother and Teddy's father came out and almost cried over him; and that night he ate all that was given him till he could eat no more, and went to bed on Teddy's shoulder, where Teddy's mother saw him when she came to look late at night.

"He saved our lives and Teddy's life," she said to her husband. "Just think, he saved all our lives."

And Rikki-Tikki kept that house and that garden as a mongoose should keep it, with tooth and jump and spring and bite, till never a cobra dared show its head inside the walls.

"Rikki-Tikki-Tavi" by Rudyard Kipling: Story Chart

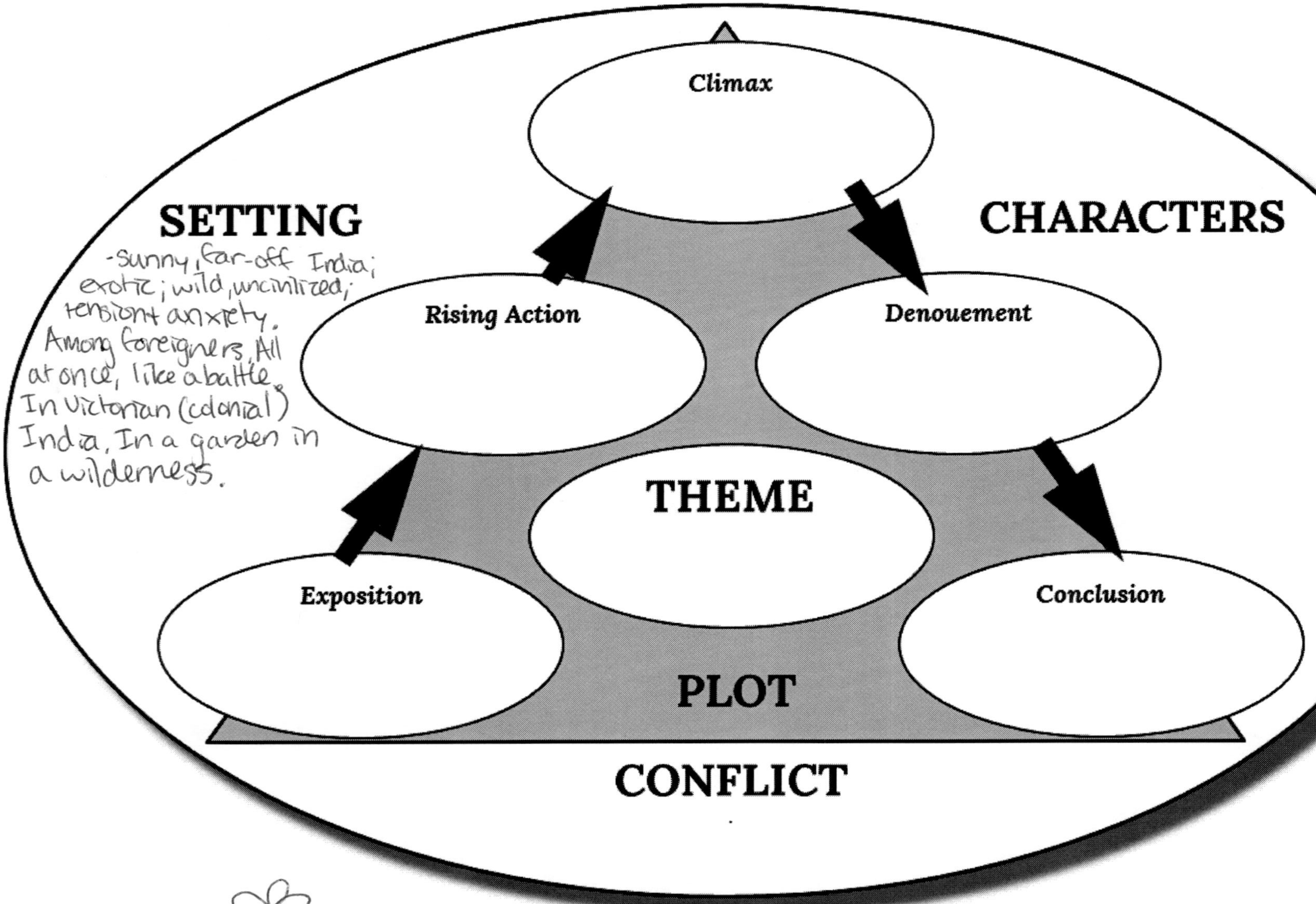

"Rikki-Tikki-Tavi" by Rudyard Kipling

Discussion Notes on Setting

Question numbers in parentheses refer to the Socratic List, included in this syllabus as Appendix A.

1. What is the mood or atmosphere of the place where the story happens? Is it cheerful and sunny, or dark and bleak? What words or phrases or descriptions does the author use to create this atmosphere? (Question 1d.)

-India
-sunny
-big bungalow - bathrooms & gardens
-exotic - bamboo, huge bushes, high grass

2. In what country or region does the story happen? How does this location contribute to the mood or atmosphere of the story? (Question 1a.)

-Segowlee province of India
-"otherness" -exotic -wild
-uncivilized / dangerous / tension & anxiety

3. Among what kinds of people is the story set? What is their economic class? How do they live? Are they hopeful? Downtrodden? Depressed? Why? (Question 1h.)

-British family - foreigners - strangers in a strange land
-

4. How long a period of time does the story cover? A few minutes? A single day? A whole lifetime? (Question 2b)

-a couple of days
-quick like a battle or war

5. Does the story happen in a particular year, era, or age of the world? What historical events may have just preceded the period of the story? Do these events help explain the actions of characters, the action of the story, or its mood? (For example, this particular story is set in the British Imperial Age when the British are colonizing Africa. This explains Teddy and his family's social position in the story. They are unwelcome strangers in a foreign land, and this social atmosphere affects even the garden and its occupants.) (Question 2d.)

- colonization of India - Queen Victoria
- trying to civilize India - garden in the wilderness
↳ fight or war

6. Does the author use sound words to tell his story? (Question 14a.)

Onomanopeia

7. Does the author use words in sequence or in close proximity that repeat the same initial consonant sound? (Question 14e.)

alliteration

8. Does the author use the words "like" or "as" in making comparisons between two or more dissimilar things? (Question 16d.)

Similes

Rikki is half wild and half civilized

9. Do things or creatures speak with human voices, expressing rational thoughts and ideas? (Question 16f.)

Yes - personification

Setting in Adult Literature

The settings of works of adult fiction are as varied, of course, as their juvenile counterparts. Some sample settings from the aforementioned classics are presented here.

The Iliad

The Iliad of Homer is the world's first great epic poem. The story takes place in the tenth year of the Trojan War on the fields between the shores of the Mediterranean Sea and the Walls of Troy. Set in the deep past where history recedes into legend and myth, the story unfolds in a time of monsters, superhuman warriors, and all-too-human deities. The poet calls attention to the gravity of his themes and the greatness of his characters by using stock epithets and epic similes. The supernatural elements of the story punctuate its monumental scope.

Macbeth

William Shakespeare's *Macbeth* is the shortest (and perhaps the bloodiest) of the playwright's ten great tragedies. The story takes place in eleventh-century Scotland, a land of foggy moors and "blasted heaths" (Macbeth 1.3.78). The action occurs between various nobles (or thanes) of the land, and many of the scenes are therefore set at court and in the various drafty castles of the Scottish nobility. The setting of the play takes on added significance when the context in which it was written is considered. King James I of England and Scotland, patron of Shakespeare's theatrical group The King's Men, reigned when the play was first performed. Allusions to his reign occur predominantly in Act 4, Scene 1. In fact, it is his august lineage the usurper Macbeth foresees in the mirror through divination. This context imbued the subject matter of the play with significance for its first audience. Much of the action of *Macbeth* takes place at night, and the prominence of witches, spells, ghosts, and visions gives the play a dark, spooky mood.

Great Expectations

The greatest novel by the greatest novelist of the Victorian age, Charles Dickens' *Great Expectations* tells the story of the career of Pip, a young orphan growing up in the home of his blacksmith brother-in-law. Set in a small village in rural England in the early nineteenth century, the story contains vivid descriptions of the people and customs that made this particular place and time so distinctive. Dickens employs simile, irony, and understatement to create some of the greatest caricatures in the history of literature, proving him one of the great humorists of the age.

To Kill a Mockingbird

Harper Lee's Pulitzer Prize winning novel chronicles a young girl coming of age in rural Alabama during the Great Depression. The story is narrated from the girl's point of view, using a brilliant combination of eight-year-old perspective and adult vocabulary that makes readers instinctively receptive to the deeply perceptive critiques of Southern social mores and racism. Lee's mastery of Southern American dialect and familiarity with the customs of that society allow her to create a believable world so that the shattering events she describes strike us as all too real.

SECTION 4:
CHARACTERS

Characters, the people in a story, are the link between the imaginary world of the author and the reader of his work. It is the strength of the characters and the author's description of them that allow the story to move us, attract or repel us, challenge and affect us. We relate to the vicissitudes of human existence. Human struggles make stories real. Character analysis is quintessential to sound story interpretation.

How do readers come to know a character, then? The author reveals him through:

- His behavior and appearance
- What he says and thinks about himself, out loud and in the privacy of his own mind
- What other characters say or think about him
- What he says and thinks about other characters
- The way he interacts with his environment – with other people and with his surroundings
- The ways he is similar to or different from the characters around him (called *juxtaposition*)

To understand a character, a reader identifies similarities and differences between himself and the literary figure. Each author asks the reader to relate to the character as if he were sitting beside him – because, of course, when he reads, he is.

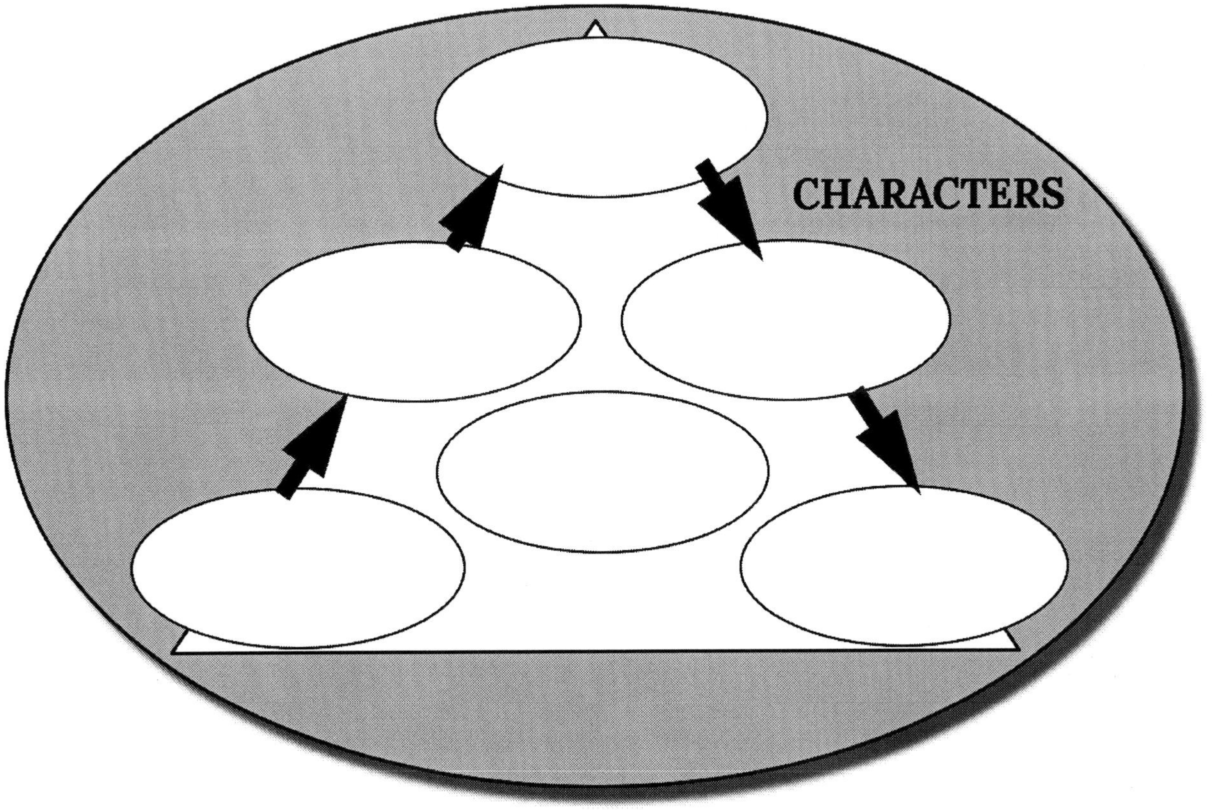

From *The Adventures of Tom Sawyer* by Mark Twain

Saturday morning was come, and all the summer world was bright and fresh, and brimming with life. There was a song in every heart; and if the heart was young the music issued at the lips. There was cheer in every face and a spring in every step. The locust-trees were in bloom and the fragrance of the blossoms filled the air. Cardiff Hill, beyond the village and above it, was green with vegetation and it lay just far enough away to seem a Delectable Land, dreamy, reposeful, and inviting.

Tom appeared on the sidewalk with a bucket of whitewash and a long-handled brush. He surveyed the fence, and all gladness left him and a deep melancholy settled down upon his spirit. Thirty yards of board fence nine feet high. Life to him seemed hollow, and existence but a burden. Sighing, he dipped his brush and passed it along the topmost plank; repeated the operation; did it again; compared the insignificant whitewashed streak with the far-reaching continent of unwhitewashed fence, and sat down on a tree-box discouraged.

Jim came skipping out at the gate with a tin pail, and singing Buffalo Gals. Bringing water from the town pump had always been hateful work in Tom's eyes, before, but now it did not strike him so. He remembered that there was company at the pump. Boys and girls were always there waiting their turns, resting, trading playthings, quarrelling, fighting, skylarking. And he remembered that although the pump was only a hundred and fifty yards off, Jim never got back with a bucket of water under an hour--and even then somebody generally had to go after him. Tom said:

"Say, Jim, I'll fetch the water if you'll whitewash some."

Jim shook his head and said:

"Can't, Mars Tom. Ole missis, she tole me I got to go an' git dis water an' not stop foolin' roun' wid anybody. She say she spec' Mars Tom gwine to ax me to whitewash, an' so she tole me go 'long an' 'tend to my own business--she 'lowed SHE'D 'tend to de whitewashin'."

"Oh, never you mind what she said, Jim. That's the way she always talks. Gimme the bucket--I won't be gone only a minute. SHE won't ever know."

"Oh, I dasn't, Mars Tom. Ole missis she'd take an' tar de head off'n me. 'Deed she would."

"SHE! She never licks anybody--whacks 'em over the head with her thimble--and who cares for that, I'd like to know. She talks awful, but talk don't hurt. Jim, I'll give you a marble. I'll give you a white alley!"

Jim began to waver.

"My! Dat's a mighty gay marble, I tell you! But Mars Tom I's powerful 'fraid ole missis-"

"And besides, if you will I'll show you my sore toe."

Jim was only human--this attraction was too much for him. He put down his pail, took the white alley, and bent over the toe with absorbing interest while the bandage was being unwound. In another moment he was flying down the street with his pail and a tingling rear, Tom was whitewashing with vigor, and Aunt Polly was retiring from the field with a slipper in her hand and triumph in her eye.

But Tom's energy did not last. He began to think of the fun he had planned for this day, and his sorrows multiplied. Soon the free boys would come tripping along on all sorts of delicious expeditions, and they would make a world of fun of him for having to work--the very thought of it burnt him like fire. He got out his worldly wealth and examined it--bits of toys, marbles, and trash; enough to buy an exchange of WORK, maybe, but not half enough to buy so much as half an hour of pure freedom. So he returned his straitened means to his pocket, and gave up the idea of trying to buy the boys.

At this dark and hopeless moment an inspiration burst upon him! Nothing less than a great, magnificent inspiration.

He took up his brush and went tranquilly to work. Ben Rogers hove in sight presently--the very boy, of all boys, whose ridicule he had been dreading. Ben's gait was the hop-skip-and-jump--proof enough that his heart was light and his anticipations high. He was eating an apple, and giving a long, melodious whoop, at intervals, followed by a deep-toned ding-dong, ding-dong, for he was personating a steamboat. As he drew near, he slackened speed, took the middle of the street, leaned far over to starboard and "rounded to" ponderously and with laborious pomp and circumstance--for he was personating the Big Missouri, and considered himself to be drawing nine feet of water. He was boat and captain and engine-bells combined, so he had to imagine himself standing on his own hurricane-deck giving the orders and executing them:

"Stop her, sir! Ting-a-ling-ling!" He drew up slowly toward the sidewalk.

"Ship up to back! Ting-a-ling-ling!" His arms straightened and stiffened down his sides.

"Set her back on the stabboard! Ting-a-ling-ling! Chow! ch-chow-wow!" His right hand described stately circles--for it was representing a forty-foot wheel.

"Stop the stabboard! Ting-a-ling-ling! Stop the labboard! Ting-a-ling-ling! Chow-ch-chow! Get out that head-line! LIVELY now! Done with the engines, sir! Ting-a-ling-ling! SH'T! S'H'T! SH'T!"

Tom went on whitewashing--paid no attention to the steamboat. Ben stared a moment and then said: "Hi-YI! YOU'RE up a stump, ain't you!"

No answer. Tom surveyed his last touch with the eye of an artist, then he gave his brush another gentle sweep and surveyed the result, as before. Ben ranged up alongside of him. Tom's mouth watered for the apple, but he stuck to his work. Ben said:

"Hello, old chap – you got to work, hey?"

Tom wheeled suddenly and said:

"Why, it's you, Ben! I warn't noticing."

"Say--I'm going in a-swimming, I am. Don't you wish you could? But of course you'd druther WORK--wouldn't you? Course you would!"

Tom contemplated the boy a bit, and said:

"What do you call work?"

"Why, ain't THAT work?"

Tom resumed his whitewashing, and answered carelessly:

"Well, maybe it is, and maybe it ain't. All I know is, it suits Tom Sawyer."

"Oh come, now, you don't mean to let on that you LIKE it?"

The brush continued to move.

"Like it? Well, I don't see why I oughtn't to like it. Does a boy get a chance to whitewash a fence every day?"

That put the thing in a new light. Ben stopped nibbling his apple. Tom swept his brush daintily back and forth--stepped back to note the effect--added a touch here and there- criticized the effect again—Ben watching every move and getting more and more interested, more and more absorbed. Presently he said:

"Say, Tom, let ME whitewash a little."

Tom considered, was about to consent; but he altered his mind:

"No--no--I reckon it wouldn't hardly do, Ben. You see, Aunt Polly's awful particular about this fence--right here on the street, you know --but if it was the back fence I wouldn't mind and SHE wouldn't. Yes, she's awful particular about this fence; it's got to be done very careful; I reckon there ain't one boy in a thousand, maybe two thousand, that can do it the way it's got to be done."

"No--is that so? Oh come, now--lemme just try. Only just a little--I'd let YOU, if you was me, Tom."

"Ben, I'd like to, honest injun; but Aunt Polly--well, Jim wanted to do it, but she wouldn't let him; Sid wanted to do it, and she wouldn't let Sid. Now don't you see how I'm fixed? If you was to tackle this fence and anything was to happen to it--"

"Oh, shucks, I'll be just as careful. Now lemme try. Say--I'll give you the core of my apple."

"Well, here--No, Ben, now don't. I'm afeard--"

"I'll give you ALL of it!"

Tom gave up the brush with reluctance in his face, but alacrity in his heart. And while the late steamer Big Missouri worked and sweated in the sun, the retired artist sat on a barrel in the shade close by, dangled his legs, munched his apple, and planned the slaughter of more innocents. There was no lack of material; boys happened along every little while; they came to jeer, but remained to whitewash. By the time Ben was fagged out, Tom had traded the next chance to Billy Fisher for a kite, in good repair; and when he played out, Johnny Miller bought in for a dead rat and a string to swing it with--and so on, and so on, hour after hour. And when the middle of the afternoon came, from being a poor poverty-stricken boy in the morning, Tom was literally rolling in wealth. He had besides the things before mentioned, twelve marbles, part of a jews-harp, a piece of blue bottle-glass to look through, a spool cannon, a key that wouldn't unlock anything, a fragment of chalk, a glass stopper of a decanter, a tin soldier, a couple of tadpoles, six fire-crackers, a kitten with only one eye, a brass doorknob, a dog-collar--but no dog--the handle of a knife, four pieces of orange-peel, and a dilapidated old window sash.

He had had a nice, good, idle time all the while--plenty of company --and the fence had three coats of whitewash on it! If he hadn't run out of whitewash he would have bankrupted every boy in the village.

Tom said to himself that it was not such a hollow world, after all. He had discovered a great law of human action, without knowing it--namely, that in order to make a man or a boy covet a thing, it is only necessary to make the thing difficult to attain. If he had been a great and wise philosopher, like the writer of this book, he would now have comprehended that Work consists of whatever a body is OBLIGED to do, and that Play consists of whatever a body is not obliged to do. And this would help him to understand why constructing artificial flowers or performing on a tread-mill is work, while rolling ten-pins or climbing Mont Blanc is only amusement.

The boy mused awhile over the substantial change which had taken place in his worldly circumstances, and then wended toward headquarters to report.

From *The Adventures of Tom Sawyer* by Mark Twain: Story Chart

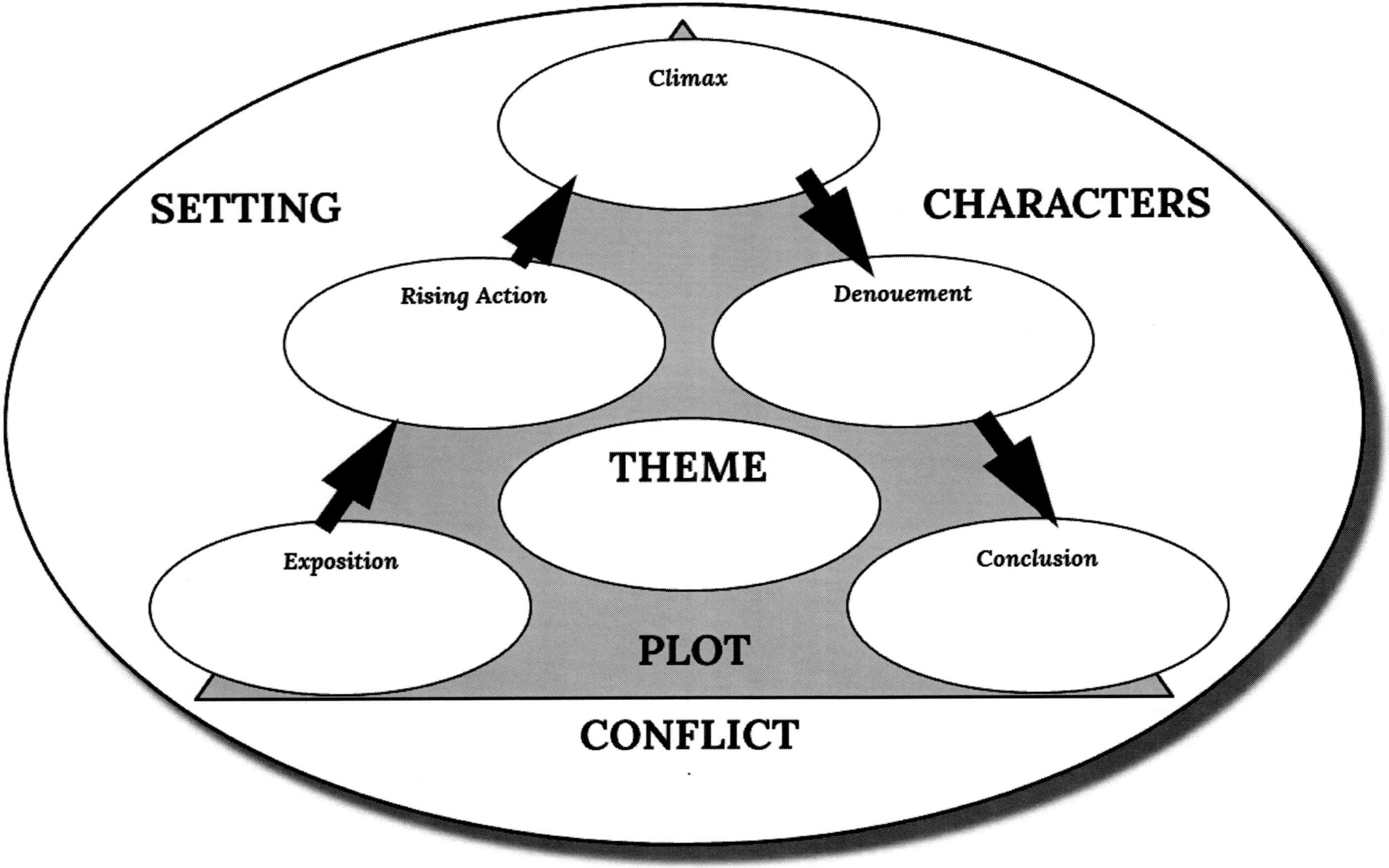

From *The Adventures of Tom Sawyer* by Mark Twain

Discussion Notes on Character

Question numbers in parentheses refer to the Socratic List, included in this syllabus as Appendix A.

1. Who is the story about? (Question 3)

2. Is the protagonist kind, gentle, stern, emotional, harsh, logical, rational, compassionate or exacting? Make up a list of adjectives that describe the protagonist. What words or actions on the protagonist's part make you choose the adjectives you do? (Question 3f.)

3. Of what nationality is the protagonist? Does he live in his native land, or somewhere else? (Question 3g.)

4. What does the character do for a living? Is he a professional, or a blue-collar worker? Is he wealthy or impoverished? Is he content with his lot in life, or does he long to improve himself, like Pip in *Great Expectations*? (Question 3h.)

5. What does the character say about himself to other people? What do his words reveal about his personality? (Question 3j.) What do other characters think or say about him? (Question 3k.)

6. What does the protagonist think is the most important thing in life? How do you know this? Does the protagonist say this out loud, or do his thoughts and actions give him away? (Question 3m.)

7. Do the protagonist's priorities change over the course of the story? In what way? What causes this change? Is it a change for the better, or for the worse? (Question 3n.)

8. Is the protagonist a type or archetype? Is he an "Everyman" with whom the reader is meant to identify? Are his struggles symbolic of human life generally in some way? (Question 3p.)

Character in Adult Literature

The Iliad: Achilles and Agamemnon

Achilles is the greatest of the Achaian warriors and is nearly invincible in battle. Agamemnon is king of the Achaians. Both men desire glory and fame (particularly the kind that is won on the battlefield) above all things. Neither will suffer hurt to his reputation, and both are prone to nurse grudges. Achilles, in particular, is given to self-pity and bitterness. Achilles is the son of a minor goddess, the sea nymph Thetis, while Agamemnon is the brother of Menelaos, whose wife, Helen, started the Trojan War by running off with Paris, the Prince of Troy. Agamemnon is frequently referred to by the epithet "wide-ruling," and Achilles often goes by "golden haired" in the text.

Macbeth: Macbeth and Lady Macbeth

Macbeth is a famous general in the service of Duncan the Meek, king of Scotland. From the very first scene, he shows himself to be susceptible to manipulation, and indeed it seems as if the outcome of the play will depend upon which character gets his (or her) hands on Macbeth last. Lady Macbeth, on the other hand, is uncommonly single-minded and relentless in pursuit of a specific goal. A Machiavellian character, she never wavers from her aim and will stop at nothing to achieve it – not even balking at a bargain with the devil. The relationship between these two main characters is a drama within the drama, as the impulses of Macbeth's fairer nature are crushed by the ambition of his wife, and his own desire for power and glory consume him.

Great Expectations: Pip and Joe Gargery

Pip is the first-person narrator of *Great Expectations*, and he is honest with the reader from the start about the failings of his own character. The novel is part morality play in which Pip uses himself as a poignant example of the immaturity of youth, the dangers of pride and selfishness, and the value of loyalty and friendship. Pip suffers from some disadvantages in the beginning of the book, but sets resolutely out to better himself as the story moves along. In the process, he becomes ashamed of Joe Gargery, his unlearned, unpretentious brother-in-law, and disregards the latter's steadfastness and constancy. Joe, the son of an abusive father, has taken a passive role in life to make certain that he doesn't follow in his father's footsteps. He persistently thinks the best of people and is willing to be inconvenienced or mistreated as long as his loved ones prosper.

To Kill a Mockingbird: Scout Finch and Boo Radley

Like Pip, Scout Finch narrates her own story, and *Mockingbird* therefore sounds like a reminiscence. The beloved daughter of a small-town lawyer, Scout is intelligent and articulate, with a keen sense of right and wrong and a hatred of injustice. Living in a world charged with racial tension and troubled by moral incongruities, Scout is forced beyond her childish perspectives to learn how to see the world from other people's points of view. In the process she leaves her childhood behind and enters the world of grown-ups. Boo Radley, on the other hand, has taken an easier path in response to similar moral incongruities. A shadowy recluse who has not left his house in years, Boo rejects human interaction altogether until he takes an interest in Scout and her brother.

SECTION 5: CONFLICT AND PLOT

The plot of a story is a simple summary of its sequence of events. Of course, every story has a beginning, a middle, and an end. To be more specific, though, every story moves through the following stages: Introduction (or Exposition), Rising Action, Climax, Dénouement (or Falling Action), and Conclusion.

In the introduction or exposition of a story, the author introduces the reader to his characters and places them in a particular scene and circumstance. This circumstance usually has the seed of a conflict within it. The rising action begins when the conflict presents and continues as events take place which cause the tension created by the conflict to grow in intensity. This tension reaches its pinnacle in the climax of the story, where the conflict is decided, for good or ill. Some people call this climactic moment the story's turning point. While the story's resolution often spills into the events of the dénouement, the real verdict of the story question is decided at the climactic moment. After the climax the story begins to "unravel," or unfold its secrets. Following the French, we call this unraveling the *dénouement*. In the conclusion, the author ties up "loose ends" for the reader or puts an interpretive spin on the story's events. For this reason the conclusion is singularly important to a conversation of the author's themes.

The *conflict* of a story is exactly what you would expect it to be, given its name: it is the tension or discord at the root of the story – the obstacle between the protagonist and his goal. In one sense, conflict is the most the essential ingredient in any story; without it, there is really no story to tell.

Every story involves or is born out of conflict, and it is often the case that widely differing interpretations of a particular work hinge upon different understandings of the nature of the central conflict.

Though there are as many conflicts as there are stories in the world, they may be grouped into a surprisingly small number of categories:

- Man versus Man
- Man versus Nature or animal
- Man versus God or Fate
- Man versus Himself
- Man versus Society

Since the conflict naturally concerns the main characters and their actions in relationship with each other, it is tied very closely to the plot of the story. You might say, in fact, that the conflict sets the plot in motion and drives it forward, giving each new event a reason for happening even as it gives the story a reason for existing in the first place. If a story is like a train, then the plot is like the tracks, and the conflict is the engine. Without the conflict, the story never goes anywhere. The solution of the conflict occurs at the climax of the story and begins its descent into dénouement and conclusion. An analysis of a story's plot (and its climax, in particular) will hinge to a great degree upon its identification of the nature of the central conflict. It is possible to construct several different story charts for a single work, each devoted to the resolution of a different conflict.

Adult literature is replete with examples of this type of complexity. *Great Expectations*, for example, can be said to contain at least three well-developed plot lines, each with its own central conflict and separate climax. The individual stories within the larger frame generally follow this plot structure internally, even as the overarching story does so externally.

As is often true, however, the relationship between plot and conflict in a story is clearest when the story has been written for children, as Beatrix Potter's *The Tale of Peter Rabbit* illustrates.

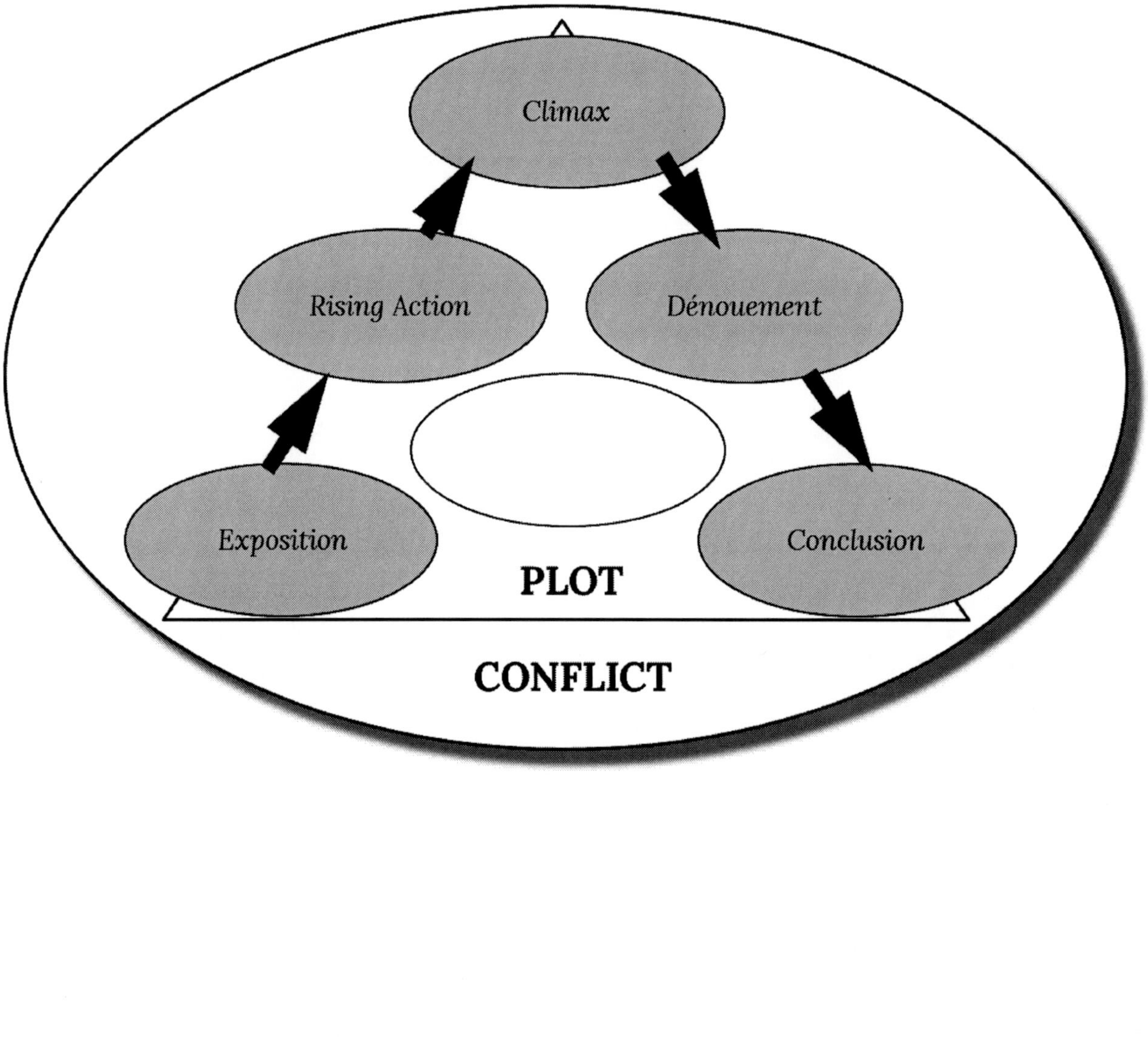

The Tale of Peter Rabbit by Beatrix Potter

Once upon a time there were four little Rabbits, and their names were-- Flopsy, Mopsy, Cotton-tail, and Peter. They lived with their Mother in a sand-bank, underneath the root of a very big fir tree.

"Now, my dears," said old Mrs. Rabbit one morning, "you may go into the fields or down the lane, but don't go into Mr. McGregor's garden: your Father had an accident there; he was put in a pie by Mrs. McGregor. Now run along, and don't get into mischief. I am going out."

Then old Mrs. Rabbit took a basket and her umbrella, to the baker's. She bought a loaf of brown bread and five currant buns.

Flopsy, Mopsy, and Cottontail, who were good little bunnies, went down the lane to gather blackberries; but Peter, who was very naughty, ran straight away to Mr. McGregor's garden and squeezed under the gate!

First he ate some lettuces and some French beans; and then he ate some radishes; and then, feeling rather sick, he went to look for some parsley.

But round the end of a cucumber frame, whom should he meet but Mr. McGregor!

Mr. McGregor was on his hands and knees planting out young cabbages, but he jumped up and ran after Peter, waving a rake and calling out, "Stop thief!"

Peter was most dreadfully frightened; he rushed all over the garden, for he had forgotten the way back to the gate.

He lost one of his shoes among the cabbages, and the other shoe amongst the potatoes.

After losing them, he ran on four legs and went faster, so that I think he might have got away altogether if he had not unfortunately run into a gooseberry net, and got caught by the large buttons on his jacket. It was a blue jacket with brass buttons, quite new.

Peter gave himself up for lost, and shed big tears; but his sobs were overheard by some friendly sparrows, who flew to him in great excitement, and implored him to exert himself.

Mr. McGregor came up with a sieve, which he intended to pop upon the top of Peter; but Peter wriggled out just in time, leaving his jacket behind him, and rushed into the tool shed, and jumped into a can. It would have been a beautiful thing to hide in, if it had not had so much water in it.

Mr. McGregor was quite sure that Peter was somewhere in the tool shed, perhaps hidden underneath a flower-pot. He began to turn them over carefully, looking under each.

Presently Peter sneezed-- "Kertyschoo!" Mr. McGregor was after him in no time, and tried to put his foot upon Peter, who jumped out of a window, upsetting three plants. The window was too small for Mr. McGregor, and he was tired of running after Peter. He went back to his work.

Peter sat down to rest; he was out of breath and trembling with fright, and he had not the least idea which way to go. Also he was very damp with sitting in that can.

After a time he began to wander about, going lippity--lippity--not very fast, and looking all around.

He found a door in a wall; but it was locked, and there was no room for a fat little rabbit to squeeze underneath.

An old mouse was running in and out over the stone doorstep, carrying peas and beans to her family in the wood. Peter asked her the way to the gate, but she had such a large pea in her mouth that she could not answer. She only shook her head at him. Peter began to cry.

Then he tried to find his way straight across the garden, but he became more and more puzzled. Presently, he came to a pond where Mr. McGregor filled his water-cans. A white cat was staring at some gold-fish; she sat very, very still, but now and then the tip of her tail twitched as if it were alive. Peter thought it best to go away without speaking to her; he had heard about cats from his cousin, little Benjamin Bunny.

He went back towards the tool-shed, but suddenly, quite close to him, he heard the noise of a hoe--scr-r-ritch, scratch, scratch, scritch. Peter scuttered underneath the bushes. But presently, as nothing happened, he came out, and climbed upon a wheelbarrow, and peeped over. The first thing he saw was Mr. McGregor hoeing onions. His back was turned towards Peter, and beyond him was the gate!

Peter got down very quietly off the wheelbarrow, and started running as fast as he could go, along a straight walk behind some black-currant bushes. Mr. McGregor caught sight of him at the corner, but Peter did not care. He slipped underneath the gate, and was safe at last in the wood outside the garden.

Mr. McGregor hung up the little jacket and the shoes for a scare-crow to frighten the blackbirds.

Peter never stopped running or looked behind him till he got home to the big fir-tree. He was so tired that he flopped down upon the nice soft sand on the floor of the rabbit-hole, and shut his eyes. His mother was busy cooking; she wondered what he had done with his clothes. It was the second little jacket and pair of shoes that Peter had lost in a fortnight!

I am sorry to say that Peter was not very well during the evening.

His mother put him to bed, and made some chamomile tea; and she gave a dose of it to Peter! "One table-spoonful to be taken at bed-time."

But Flopsy, Mopsy, and Cotton-tail had bread and milk and blackberries for supper.

The Tale of Peter Rabbit by Beatrix Potter: Story Chart

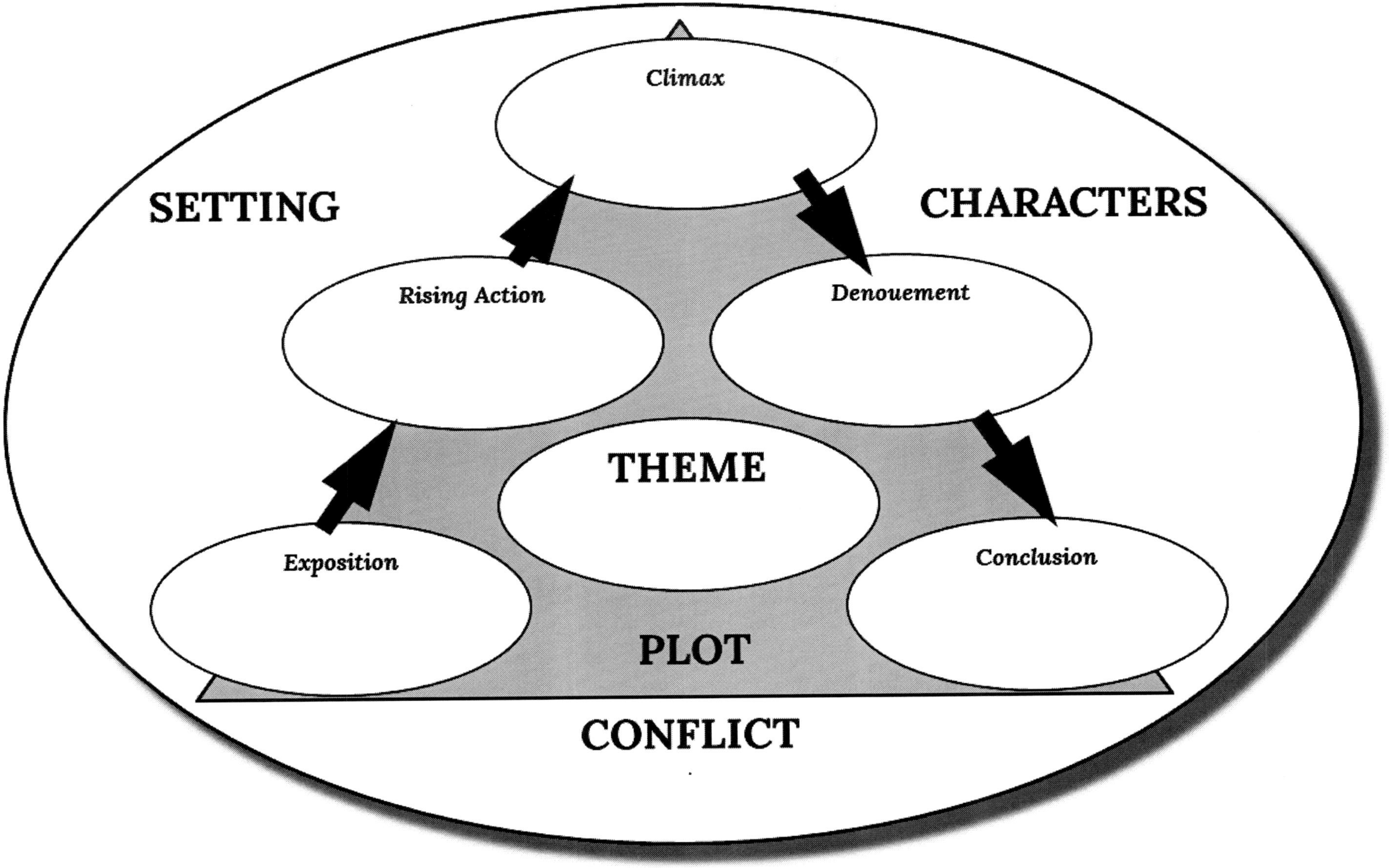

The Tale of Peter Rabbit by Beatrix Potter

Discussion Notes on Plot and Conflict

Question numbers in parentheses refer to the Socratic List, included in this syllabus as Appendix A.

1. What does the protagonist want? (Question 5)

2. Why can't he have what he wants? (Question 6)

3. What major events take place in the story as a result of this conflict? (Question 8a.)

4. Does the protagonist get what he is after? (Question 9a.)

5. Is the situation pleasantly resolved, or is it resolved in a terrible way? (Question 9c.)

6. What events form the highest point or climax of the story's tension? Are they circumstantial events, or emotional ones? Is the climax a spiritual or physical one? (Question 9d.)

7. Does the protagonist solve his own dilemma? Is it solved by some external source or third party? Is he helpless in the end to achieve his goal (like Frodo in *Lord of the Rings*), or does he triumph by virtue of his own efforts (Odysseus in *The Odyssey*)? (Question 9e.)

8. Were you satisfied with the resolution of the story? If not, why not? (Question 10b.)

9. Do you believe the characters' responses to the cataclysmic events, or are they anti-climactic in some regard? (Question 10c.)

10. Does the ending or resolution of the story make any kind of judgments? Does the resolution offer any perspective or understanding of the story's themes? (Question 10e.)

Plot and Conflict in Adult Literature

Plot structures in adult literature can be considerably more complex, of course, than those in children's books. A classic novel, for example, often contains several different plot lines that proceed at the same time toward a grand conclusion. Each individual plot may be arranged on the story chart. Plot structures for four classic works are presented on the next few pages.

The Iliad

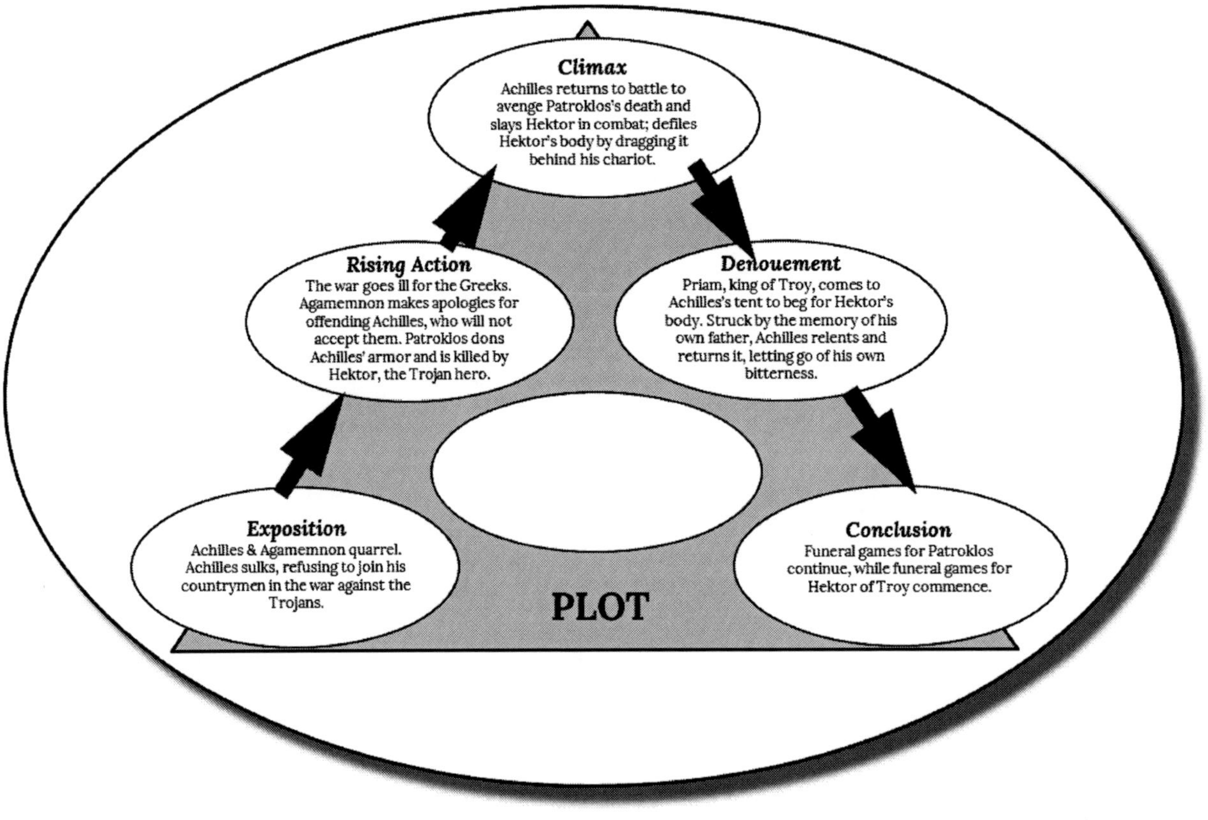

Conflicts in *The Iliad:*

Greeks vs. Trojans (Man vs. Man) – Who will keep Helen?

Achilles vs. Agamemnon (Man vs. Man) – Who will win the battle of wills?

Achilles vs. Fate (Man vs. God) – Can Achilles overcome his doom and triumph at Troy?

Achilles vs. Himself (Man vs. Himself) – Will Achilles be destroyed by his own bitterness?

Macbeth

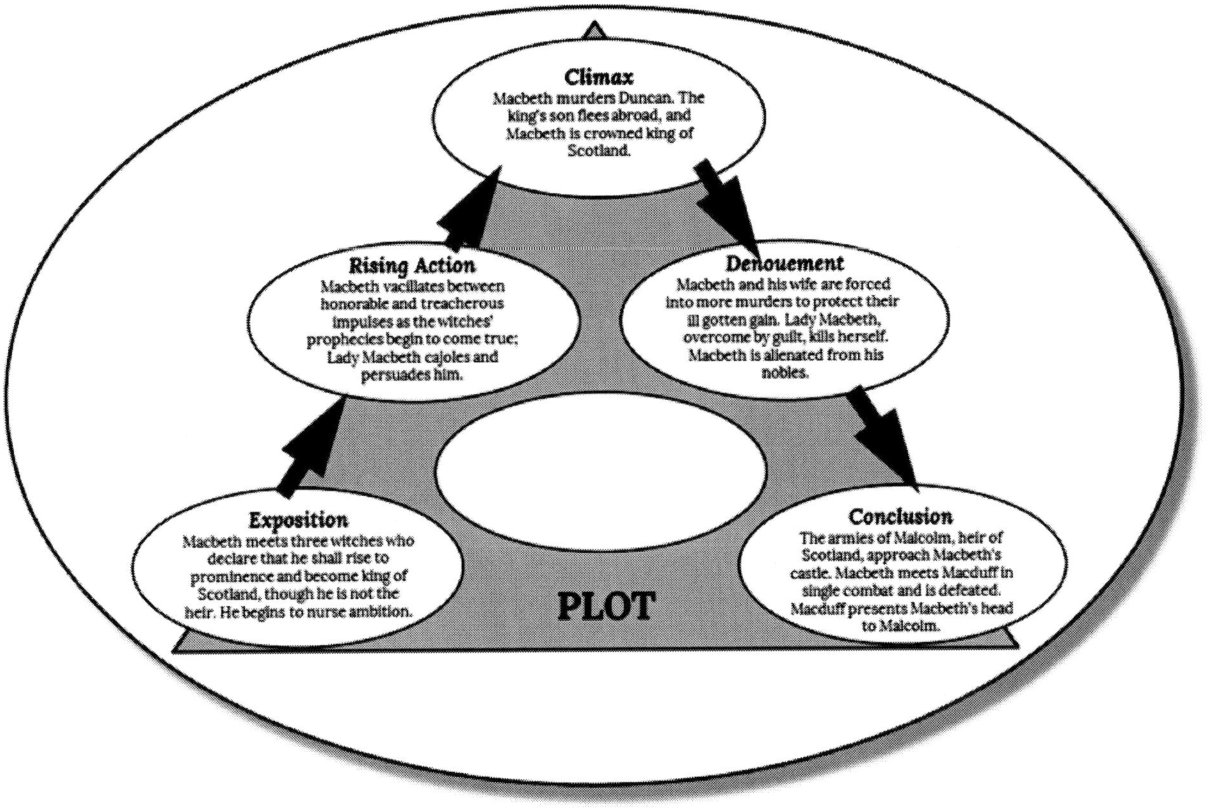

Conflicts in *Macbeth*:

Macbeth vs. Duncan's family (Man vs. Man) – Who will rule Scotland?

Macbeth vs. Lady Macbeth (Man vs. Man) – Who will rule Macbeth himself?

Macbeth vs. His Own Ambition (Man vs. Himself) – Can Macbeth resist his darker urges?

Macbeth vs. Fate (Man vs. God) – Can Macbeth choose at all?

Important Note: One of the most powerful teaching opportunities in literary interpretation occurs when different opinions arise as to how to arrange the elements of a story. Where to locate the climax of a plot line, for example, is a question that often gives rise to extremely productive discussions. The plot of Shakespeare's *Macbeth* can be understood to reach its climax at the murder of King Duncan (as shown above), or at the final battle between Macbeth and Macduff, or even at the moment in Act One when Macbeth first entertains ambitions of royalty. The important thing is to encourage your students to make an informed decision and then be ready to give the reasons for that decision. This is critical thinking!

Great Expectations

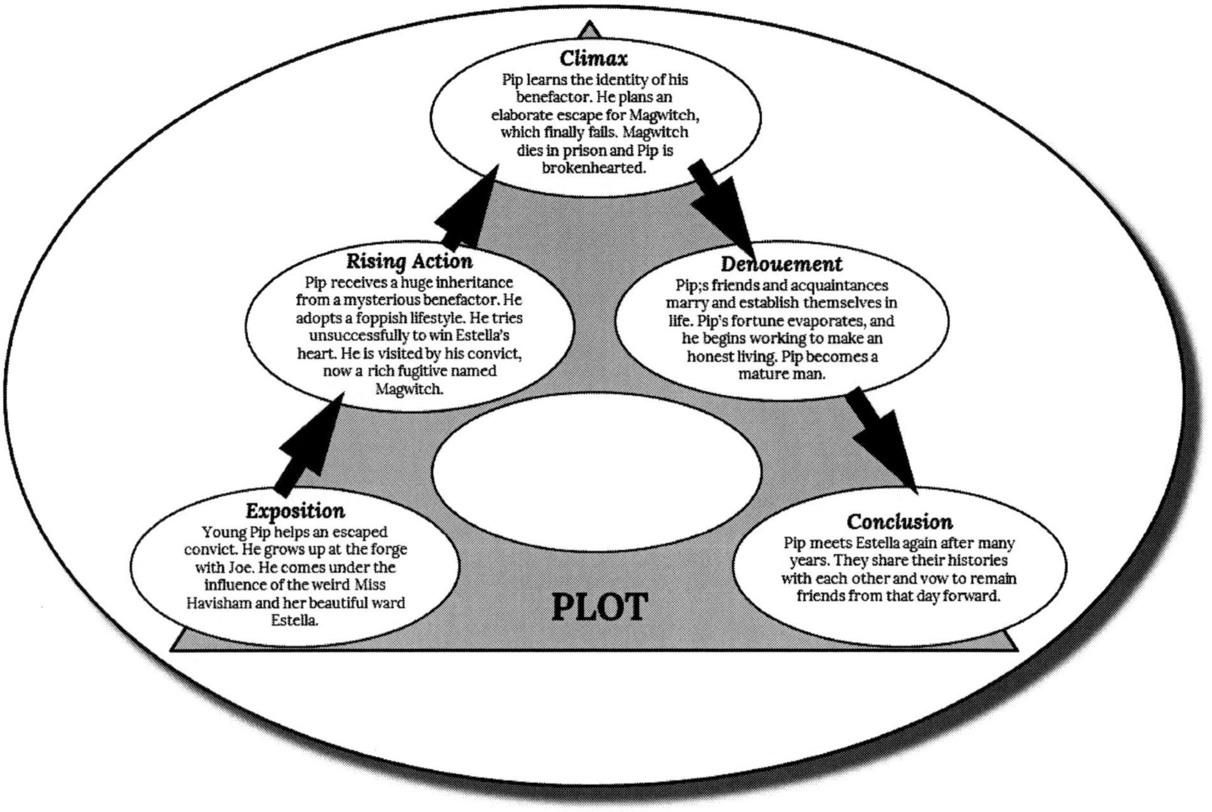

Conflicts in *Great Expectations:*

Pip vs. the Convict (Man vs. Man) – Will Pip's encounter with the convict haunt him forever?

Pip vs. Estella (Man vs. Man) – Will Pip succumb to Estella's harsh treatment/manipulation?

Pip vs. His Benefactor (Man vs. Man) – Can Pip learn the identity of his benefactor?

Pip vs. Himself #1 (Man vs. Himself) – Can Pip better himself and live up to "expectations?" Can he become a gentleman?

Pip vs. Himself #2 (Man vs. Himself) – Can Pip overcome his immaturity and selfishness? Will he discover the meaning of the word *gentleman* in his quest to become one?

To Kill a Mockingbird

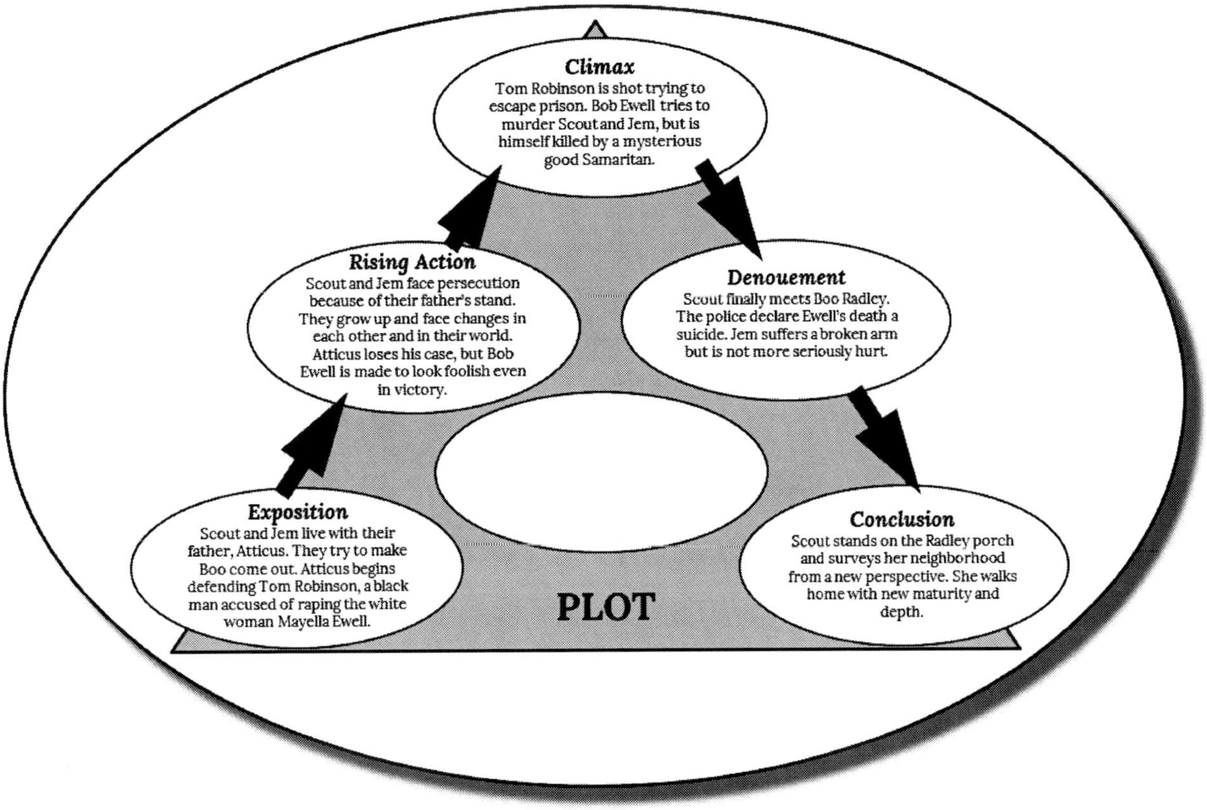

Conflicts in *To Kill a Mockingbird:*

Mayella (& Bob) Ewell vs. Tom Robinson (Man vs. Man) – Who will win in court?

Scout and Jem vs. Boo Radley (Man vs. Man) – Will the children make Boo come out?

Atticus vs. the Town (Man vs. Man) – Will Atticus be vindicated for his noble efforts?

Scout's Innocence vs. Growing Up (Man vs. Nature) – What price will Scout pay for wisdom?

"Mockingbirds" vs. "Hunters" (Man vs. Man) – Can mockingbirds ever survive? What is to become of the innocent?

SECTION 6:
THEME

The theme of a story is the underlying idea or philosophy with which the story grapples. Often (though not always) the author will articulate a particular opinion or perspective concerning that idea, which becomes part of the theme as well.

It is important to distinguish the idea of theme from some similar concepts. First, the theme of a work is not the same as the subject of the work. While the subject may be compared to the parts of a telephone – dial, mouthpiece, receiver – the theme corresponds to the idea behind the telephone, which is communication. Similarly, the subject of Dickens' *Great Expectations* is the career of its main character, while its various themes include the deceitfulness of ambition, the value of loyalty and the hypocrisy of prejudice.

One reason why the great works of Western literature have endured in popularity and influence down through the centuries is that they deal with themes which are relevant to human experience in every age of the world. Though often written about strange times and strange people, they have the power to move us because they wrestle with questions that trouble us, too.

Some Universal Themes

Prejudice
Betrayal
Innocence
Materialism vs. Idealism
Generosity of Human Nature
Wisdom of Age
Pride and Humility
Alienation
Ambition
Authority
Family Relationships
Good vs. Evil
Growing Up/Coming of Age
Fear
Honor
Survival
Loyalty
Struggles with the Conscience
Disillusionment
Compromise
Human Integrity
Human Frailty
Youth vs. Age
The Nature of Faith
The Nature of God
Innocence vs. Experience

Also important to remember is that the theme of a story is not the same as the moral of the story. Not all stories are written to teach a moral lesson, and it is not necessary that they do. There is a crucial difference, after all, between a sermon and a story. Both are good, but it is not necessary that every piece of writing be a sermon in order to be good, true, and beautiful. Though not all books have a moral, almost all have a theme of some kind. An author does not have to have complete answers to life's questions before he writes his book. Some authors ask more questions than they give answers. If properly trained, a reader will recognize the questions and after considering the author's perspective regarding them, will be moved to consider them from his own perspective. When this happens, the author has succeeded in drawing the reader into the conversation he hoped to occasion with his story. Often the most powerful thematic works do no more than hint at the author's perspective. In literature as in teaching, a well-placed question is sometimes more eloquent than the deepest sermon.

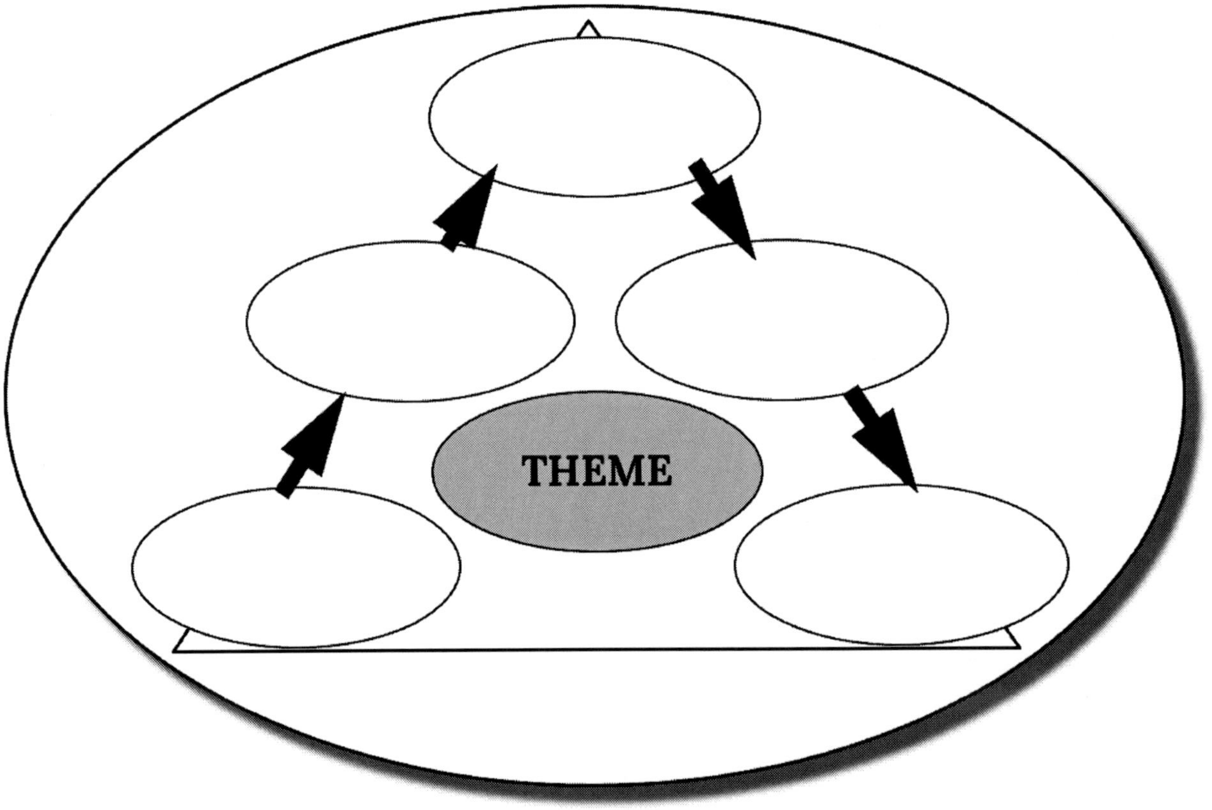

“Martin the Cobbler” by Leo Tolstoy

Adapted by Adam Andrews

In a certain town there lived a cobbler by the name of Martin. He had a tiny room in a basement, the one window of which looked out on to the street. Through it one could only see the feet of those who passed by, but Martin recognized the people by their boots. There was hardly a pair of boots in the neighborhood that had not been once or twice through his hands, so he often saw his own handiwork through the window.

One evening when he had finished his day’s work, he took the lamp down from the wall, fetched his Testament from the shelf, and sat down to read. He read about the rich man who invited Christ into his home.

“Suppose Christ came to visit me?” Martin thought to himself. “How would I welcome him?” Then Martin laid his head upon both his arms and, before he was aware of it, he fell asleep.

“Martin!” he suddenly heard a voice, as if someone had breathed the word above his ear.

He started from his sleep. “Who’s there?” he asked.

He turned round and looked at the door; no one was there. He called again. Then he heard quite distinctly: “Martin, Martin! Look out into the street tomorrow, for I shall come.”

Next morning he rose before daylight, and sat down by the window to his work. As he sat working Martin thought over what had happened the night before. At times it seemed to him like a dream, and at times he thought that he had really heard the voice of Christ. “Such things have happened before now,” thought he.

So he sat by the window, looking out into the street, and whenever anyone passed in unfamiliar boots he would stoop and look up, so as to see the face of the passer-by. Presently an old soldier came near the window, spade in hand. Martin knew him by his boots, which were shabby old felt ones, galoshed with leather. The old man was called Stepánitch. He began to clear away the snow before Martin’s window. Martin glanced at him and then went on with his work.

“I must be growing crazy with age,” said Martin, laughing at his fancy. “Stepánitch comes to clear away the snow, and I must needs imagine it’s Christ coming to visit me. Old dotard that I am!”

Yet he looked out of the window again. He saw that Stepánitch was old and broken down, and had evidently not enough strength even to clear away the snow.

Martin tapped the window with his fingers, and beckoned to Stepánitch. “Come in,” he said, “and warm yourself a bit. I’m sure you must be cold.”

“May God bless you!” Stepánitch answered. “My bones do ache to be sure.” He came in, shaking off the snow from his shabby old felt boots.

Filling two tumblers with tea from the samovar, Martin passed one to his visitor. But while he drank his tea Martin kept looking out into the street, expecting the dear Lord.

Stepánitch went away; and Martin sat down again to his work, stitching the seam of a boot. And as he stitched he kept looking out of the window, waiting for Christ to come to him.

Two soldiers went by: one in government boots, and the other in shining galoshes. Then a woman came up in peasant-made shoes. She passed the window, but stopped by the wall. Martin glanced up at her through the window, and saw that she was a stranger, poorly dressed, and with a baby in her arms. She hunched against the wall with her back to the wind, trying to wrap the baby up, though she had hardly anything to wrap it in. The woman had only summer clothes on, and even they were shabby and worn. Through the window Martin heard the baby crying. He rose, and going out of the door and up the steps, he called to her.

"Why do you stand out there with the baby in the cold?" he said. "Come inside. You can wrap him up better in a warm place!"

The woman was surprised to see the old man, but she followed him in.

"Sit down, my dear, near the stove, and warm yourself," said Martin. He brought out a basin of cabbage soup and some bread. "Sit down and eat, my dear, and I'll mind the baby. Why, bless me, I've had children of my own; I know how to manage them."

The woman began to eat, while Martin held the baby in his arms. When she had finished, she came and took the child, and Martin got up. He went and looked among some things that were hanging on the wall, and brought back an old cloak.

"Here," he said, "though it's a worn-out old thing, it will do to wrap him up in. Take it, for Christ's sake."

After the woman had gone, Martin cleared the things away, and sat down to work again. But he did not forget the window, and every time a shadow fell on it he looked up at once to see who was passing. People he knew and strangers passed by, but no one remarkable.

After a while Martin saw an apple-woman stop just in front of his window. She had a large sack full of apples on her back, which she was just setting down so that she could rest. While she was doing this a boy in a tattered cap ran up, snatched an apple out of the sack, and tried to slip away; but the old woman caught him by his sleeve. She began pulling the boy's hair and scolding him, threatening to take him to the police.

Martin ran out the door and up the stairs to the street, where he separated them. He took the boy by the hand and said, "Let him go, Granny. Forgive him for Christ's sake. He won't do it again. For Christ's sake, let him go!"

The old woman let go, and the boy wished to run away, but Martin stopped him.

"Ask the Granny's forgiveness!" said he. "And don't do it another time. I saw you take the apple."

The boy began to cry and to beg pardon.

"God bids us forgive," said Martin to the woman, "or else we shall not be forgiven. Forgive every one; and a thoughtless youngster most of all."

The old woman wagged her head and sighed. "Of course, it was only his childishness, God help him," said she.

As the old woman was about to hoist her sack on her back, the lad sprang forward to her, saying, "Let me carry it for you, Granny. I'm going that way." So the old woman put the sack on the boy's back, and they went down the street together.

When they were out of sight Martin went back to the house, sat down at his table and lit his lamp, for the day was waning. He opened his Testament and began to read, and his yesterday's dream came back to his mind. "Old dotard that I am," he thought to himself. "To imagine that Christ would really come to visit me!"

But no sooner had he thought of it than he seemed to hear footsteps, as though some one were moving behind him. Martin turned round, and it seemed to him as if people were standing in the dark corner, though he could not make out who they were. And a voice whispered in his ear: "Martin, Martin, don't you know me?"

"Who is it?" muttered Martin.

"It is I," said the voice. And out of the dark corner stepped Stepánitch, who smiled and vanishing like a cloud was seen no more.

"It is I," said the voice again. And out of the darkness stepped the woman with the baby in her arms and the woman smiled and the baby laughed, and they too vanished.

"It is I," said the voice once more. And the old woman and the boy with the apple stepped out and both smiled, and then they too vanished.

And Martin's soul grew glad. He crossed himself, put on his spectacles and began reading the Gospel just where it had opened; and at the top of the page he read:

"I was hungry, and you gave me meat: I was thirsty, and you gave me drink: I was a stranger, and you took me in."

And at the bottom of the page he read:

"Inasmuch as you did it unto one of the least of these my brethren, you did it unto me." And Martin understood that his dream had come true; and that the Savior had really come to him that day, and he had welcomed him.

“Martin the Cobbler” by Leo Tolstoy: Story Chart

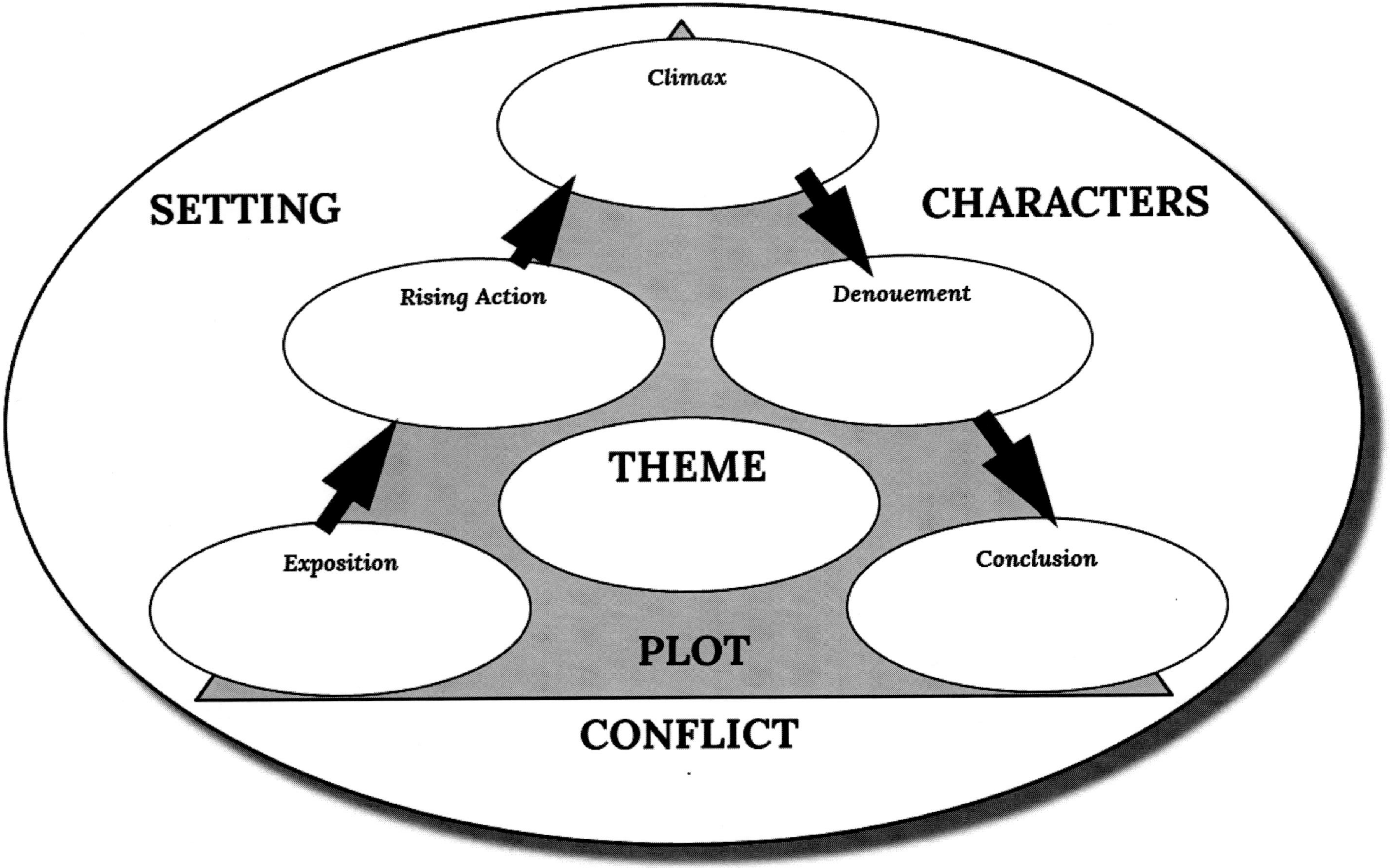

"Martin the Cobbler" by Leo Tolstoy

Discussion Notes on Theme

Question numbers in parentheses refer to the Socratic List, included in this syllabus as Appendix A.

1. Among what kinds of people is the story set? What is their economic class? How do they live? Are they hopeful? Downtrodden? Depressed? Why? (Question 1h.)

2. In what time of life for the main characters do the events occur? Are they children? Are they just passing into adulthood? Are they already grownups? Does setting the story in this particular time of the characters' lives make the story better? (Question 2e.)

3. What is the weather like in the story? (Question 1e.)

4. Is the character kind, gentle, stern, emotional, harsh, logical, rational, compassionate or exacting? Make up a list of adjectives that describe the protagonist. What words or actions on the character's part make you choose the adjectives you do? (Question 3f.)

5. What does the protagonist think is the most important thing in life? How do you know this? Does the protagonist say this out loud, or do his thoughts and actions give him away? (Question 3m.)

6. What does the protagonist want? Fill in the blank: This story is about the protagonist trying to ________. (Question 5a.)

7. How is the main problem solved? Does the protagonist get what he is after? (9a.) How are the protagonist's obstacles finally overcome? (9b.) What events form the highest point or climax of the story's tension? (9d.)

8. What does the protagonist learn? Does he begin to act differently? In what way? (Question 11b.)

9. Is he changed in his mind or heart by the events of the story? (Question 11a.)

10. Does the story seem to deal with one of the universal themes listed in Section 6 of this syllabus? (Question 13a.) If so, what does the author suggest about this idea?

11. Does the author refer to other works of literature, historical events, works of art, or well-known ideas in his work? (Question 17f.)

12. Do you know more about the character than the character himself does at any point in the story (dramatic irony)? (Question 17e.)

13. Does the story merely call the reader's attention to a theme without trying to solve anything? (Question 13c.)

Theme in Adult Literature

A partial list of themes in the four adult works we have studied is presented here. Notice the relatively small number of themes addressed by these widely disparate works. Though they have little in common in terms of genre, style, subject matter or historical context, they all deal with similar themes! This is a clue to the mystery of "the classic."

The Iliad

The Devastating Effects of Bitterness

The Limitations of Free Will and Superiority of Fate

The Importance of Loyalty and Friendship

The Love of Fathers for Their Sons

Macbeth

Ambition and Its Consequences

The Consequences of Treachery and Betrayal

The Significance of Guilt and Remorse

The Interplay of Man's Free Will and Fate

Great Expectations

Lost Innocence/Coming of Age

Ambition and Its Consequences

The Goodness of Loyalty and Friendship

The Consequences of Treachery and Betrayal

The Immaturity of Youth

The Power of Kindness and Self-Sacrifice

To Kill a Mockingbird

Lost Innocence

The Power of Kindness and Self-Sacrifice

The Brotherhood of Man

Good versus Evil

SECTION 7:
PRACTICUM

"Casey at the Bat" by Ernest Lawrence Thayer

(A Ballad of the Republic. Sung in the Year 1888.)

The outlook wasn't brilliant for the Mudville nine that day;
The score stood four to two with but one inning more to play.
And then when Cooney died at first, and Barrows did the same,
A sickly silence fell upon the patrons of the game.

A straggling few got up to go in deep despair. The rest
Clung to that hope which springs eternal in the human breast;
They thought if only Casey could but get a whack at that --
We'd put up even money now with Casey at the bat.

But Flynn preceded Casey, as did also Jimmy Blake.
And the former was a lulu and the latter was a cake;
So upon that stricken multitude grim melancholy sat.
For there seemed but little chance of Casey's getting to the bat.

But Flynn let drive a single, to the wonderment of all,
And Blake, the much despised, tore the cover off the ball;
And when the dust had lifted, and the men saw what had occurred,
There was Jimmy safe at second and Flynn a-hugging third.

Then from five thousand throats and more there rose a lusty yell;
It rumbled through the valley, it rattled in the dell;
It knocked upon the mountain and recoiled upon the flat,
For Casey, mighty Casey, was advancing to the bat.

There was ease in Casey's manner as he stepped into his place,
There was pride in Casey's bearing and a smile on Casey's face.
And when, responding to the cheers, he lightly doffed his hat,
No stranger in the crowd could doubt 'twas Casey at the bat.

Ten thousand eyes were on him as he rubbed his hands with dirt;
Five thousand tongues applauded when he wiped them on his shirt.
Then while the writhing pitcher ground the ball into his hip,
Defiance gleamed in Casey's eye, a sneer curled Casey's lip.

And now the leather-covered sphere came hurtling through the air,
And Casey stood a-watching it in haughty grandeur there.
Close by the sturdy batsman the ball unheeded sped --
"That ain't my style," said Casey. "Strike one," the umpire said.

From the benches, black with people, there went up a muffled roar,
Like the beating of the storm waves on a worn and distant shore.
"Kill him! Kill the umpire!" shouted someone in the stands,
And it's likely they'd have done it had not Casey raised his hand.

With a smile of Christian charity great Casey's visage shone;
He stilled the rising tumult; he bade the game go on;
He signaled to the pitcher and once more the spheroid flew;
But Casey still ignored it and the umpire said, "Strike two."

"Fraud!" cried the maddened thousands, and echo answered “Fraud!”
But one scornful look from Casey and the audience was awed.
They saw his face grow stern and cold, they saw his muscles strain,
And they knew that Casey wouldn't let that ball go by again.

The sneer is gone from Casey's lip, his teeth are clenched in hate;
He pounds with cruel violence his bat upon the plate.
And now the pitcher holds the ball and now he lets it go,
And now the air is shattered by the force of Casey's blow.

Oh! Somewhere in this favored land the sun is shining bright;
The band is playing somewhere, and somewhere hearts are light,
And somewhere men are laughing, and somewhere children shout;
But there is no joy in Mudville – mighty Casey has struck out.

"Casey at the Bat" by Ernest Lawrence Thayer: Story Chart

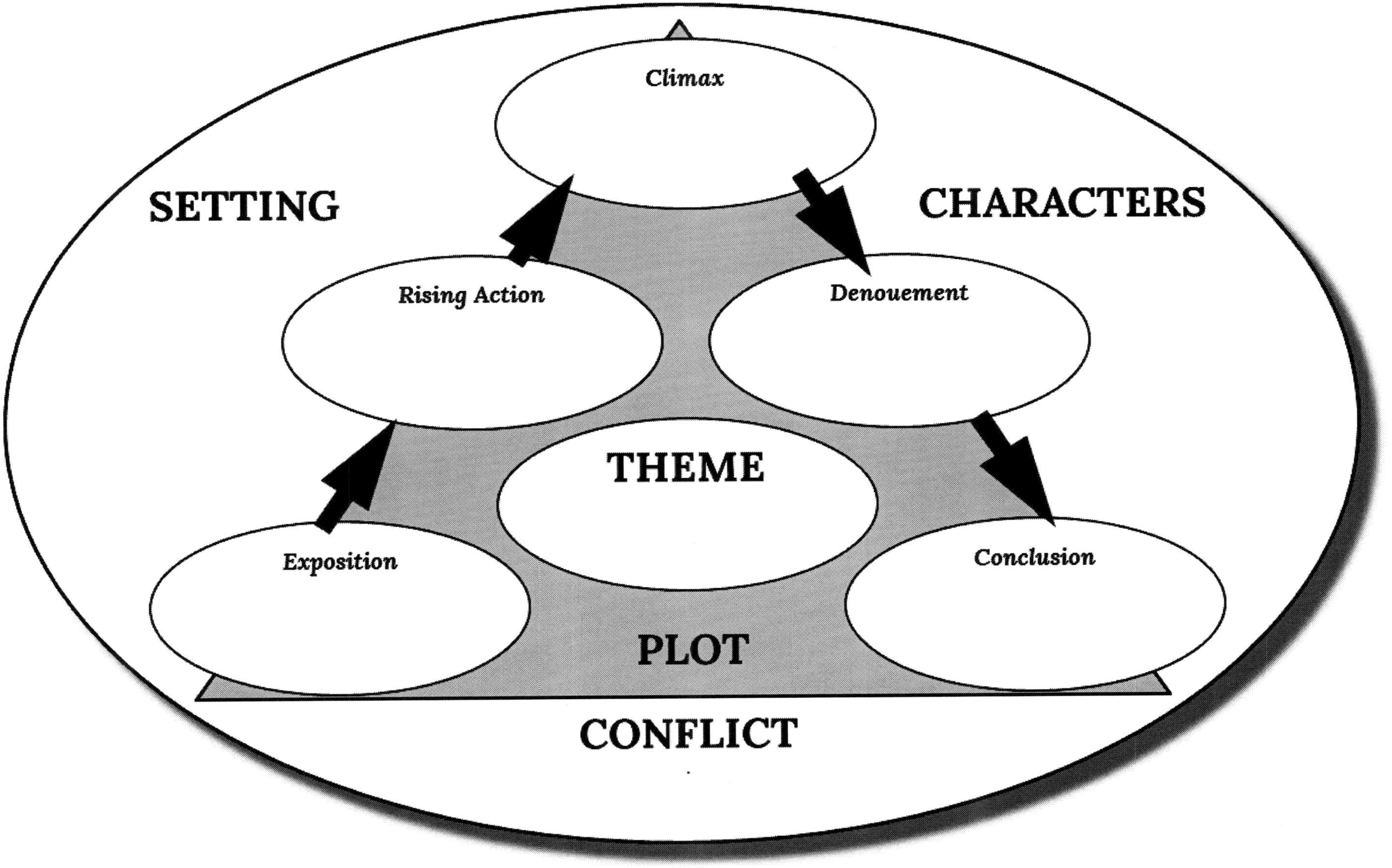

“Casey at the Bat” by Ernest Lawrence Thayer

Discussion Notes

"Casey at the Bat" by Ernest Lawrence Thayer

Discussion Notes

"Casey at the Bat" by Ernest Lawrence Thayer

Discussion Notes

SECTION 8:
A CURRICULUM FOR LITERATURE

Scope and Sequence

The habits of reading which this seminar presents can be learned by even the youngest students. The best way to introduce this program is to do exactly what we have done in this seminar: start with children's books, *regardless of the age of the student.* Use a separate children's book or two to present each structural element of fiction. Present the structural elements one at a time and repeat the process to focus attention on the stylistic devices addressed in this seminar and to emphasize issues of historical context when relevant. Once the individual elements of fiction are familiar, it will be appropriate to discuss all five elements as well as several stylistic devices for *each* book assigned.

The first month of the school year might thus be taken up with bi-weekly lessons focused on learning the five elements of fiction and the stylistic devices. On or around the beginning of the sixth week, the basic techniques of this program should be familiar to most upper level students, and they may begin reading and analyzing works of literature at their own reading levels, as in the following example, developed for a high school aged traditional day school student:

Week	Lesson (Structure – Style)	Stories
1	Setting – Personification, Imagery	"Rikki-Tikki-Tavi"
2	Character – Irony, Foreshadowing	*Tom Sawyer*
3	Conflict and Plot – Alliteration, Rhyme	*Peter Rabbit,* "Paul Revere's Ride"
4	Theme – Allusion	"Martin the Cobbler"
5	(Reading Only)	*Huckleberry Finn*
6	Setting and Character – Alliteration, Irony	*Huckleberry Finn*
7	Conflict and Plot – Understatement	*Huckleberry Finn*
8	Theme – Imagery, Allusion	*Huckleberry Finn*
9	Context and Authorship	*Huckleberry Finn*

Once students become familiar with the structural elements of a story, it is appropriate to have them read books in their entirety before attempting a formal discussion. Authors intend their books to be experienced as a complete work of art. Any classes during the reading period ought to focus predominantly upon careful reading with student and teacher reading significant passages aloud, giving attention to detail and noticing literary devices and syntax. In addition, contextual information regarding the author and his period fit neatly into this time frame. After the student has enjoyed the story in its entirety, it is time for more formal analysis. Most stories can be profitably discussed in this manner during the course of a two-hour class.

Once learned, the techniques of literary analysis presented in this seminar can be applied over and over to every work of fiction. Thus, the only limit to the number of books that may be included in an academic year is the ability and willingness of the student (and the teacher!) to read with attention and comprehension. It will be impossible for one student to read all of the great books of Western civilization (or even of the English language) in a single lifetime; therefore, it is wise to set your sights somewhat lower! Read and assign as many or as few as you like.

This program aspires to teach a habit of mind through Socratic discussion of the structure and stylistic devices of stories. We firmly believe that once students are trained to think about literature Socratically, they will continue to do so without prompting. For this reason, how they learn to think about the books they read is of more significance than how many books they cover in a given year. One book read well trumps many read poorly. Set realistic goals when planning your reading list. Leave plenty of time for slow reading and discussion.

We suggest composing a rather long list of quality books for student selected, self-directed reading. Require a certain number of these to be read in addition to the books you will be studying formally together. The student should be encouraged to read for pleasure, without having always to feel the pressure of formal discussion and analysis. A love of reading is the ultimate goal of this approach to literature. The study techniques outlined in this seminar are designed to encourage this, but you can easily burn a student out by making every book an assignment.

Reading Lists

See Appendix B of this syllabus for a starter list of high quality literature. In addition, Center For Lit publishes *Reading Roadmaps*, a K-12 scope and sequence complete with annotated reading lists for every grade level. More information about *Reading Roadmaps* can be found at www.centerforlit.com.

Other quality booklists include:

- *Books Children Love*, by Elizabeth Wilson
- *Let the Authors Speak*, by Carolyn Hatcher
- *Honey for a Child's Heart*, by Gladys Hunt
- *Who Should We Then Read*, by Jan Bloom
- *The Book Tree*, by Elizabeth McCallum and Jane Scott

These books can provide parents peace of mind in a sea of books that may be undesirable. It is impossible to pre-read every book your speedy reader wishes to plow through! Find a book list whose author you trust, and armed with your list, navigate the sea of options at your local library, avoiding the sharks and rays that crowd the shelves there.

Daily Lesson Plans

IMPORTANT: It is not necessary that a formal literature lesson happen every day. Formal discussion of literature should be mixed into the curriculum with informal reading for pleasure.

Once you have introduced the five elements of fiction one at a time to your students, you are ready to tackle books as full-orbed literary units. Teaching a particular book will involve the same lesson plan for every student, regardless of his age and ability level. He will (a) read the book; (b) take notes on a story chart during a discussion or two with the teacher (or, in the case of younger students, participate in an oral question and answer session); and (c) write on some aspect of the book at his own writing level and stage of development. Thus the teacher will make three assignments for each work, only one of which will require class time dedicated solely to the literature course.

A. Assign the reading.

Reading time should of course be scheduled for younger students, and we encourage using class time for silent reading. Often the structured environment of the classroom (or kitchen table!) is the best atmosphere for reading, because the student, in the absence of other opportunities, may concentrate more fully on the book. We also favor having the student read the book in its entirety before requiring him to do "exercises" upon it. The techniques of the Teaching the Classics approach, in particular, are most easily practiced upon a book the student has just completed.

Note on assignments: Once the student is able to read "chapter books" on his own, he can be given a full week or even more to finish a reading assignment. Nothing will be lost by allowing him to finish the book in his own time rather than racing him through it for the sake of making progress through a booklist (provided, of course, that he is applying himself consistently to the task!).

B. Schedule class discussions.

Schedule two or three discussions about the book, preferably in the same week (Tuesday and Thursday; or Monday, Wednesday and Friday, for example). The goal for these discussions will be to create a story worksheet through use of the Socratic List, described above. Older students may be able to accomplish the discussion in a single lengthy class.

Before discussions begin it is crucial to remember this cardinal principle of teaching literature: The teacher must have *read* the book he is discussing! He must also have *asked* and *answered* each of the questions he will put to his students, and he must have *located examples* in the text for each point. In this way the students will be guided by example through the process to become better readers and thinkers.

Suggested Class Discussion Procedures:

- Before the lesson, select a series of questions from the Socratic List appropriate to the age and experience of the students, and to the particular qualities of the assigned book. Choose questions which relate to the specific elements of fiction that you want to focus on that day: Setting, Characters, Plot, Conflict, or Theme. (If you have scheduled two discussions for the week, you might cover Setting and Character the first day, and save the other three for the next day. A three-session week might take two elements at a time and save the Theme for the last day.)
- Write the questions on the board one at a time. Collect answers from the class for each of the questions. Write the answers on the board and discuss them with the class.
- Have students arrange their answers on the story worksheet (see next page).

Important: It is not intended that the Socratic List be photocopied and passed out to every student as a worksheet. The Socratic List should be thought of as the teacher's weapon for waging class discussion. It is his cheat sheet; his store of provocative questions with which to spark the imaginations of his students. It is not an assignment! Students do not even need to see it. Their job is the reading, the discussion/story chart, and the essay/oral presentation.

C. Assign a writing exercise.

At the final discussion, make the writing assignment, which could be due in rough draft form the next day for grammar level students who are writing a paragraph at a time, in two or three days' time for logic level students, or the following week for rhetoric level students.

The Socratic List should provide a good source for writing assignment ideas as well as a way to "seed the clouds" for a brainstorm. As with all writing assignments, student essays should periodically be read aloud to the class, the parents, or the family as an aid to training in the art of public speaking.

Depending upon the age and ability of your students, choose writing assignments such as the ones from the following lists.

Grammar Level Writing Assignments:

- Three point paragraphs on the plot of the story, which may be expanded into three paragraph essays as the student matures
- Key thought outline summaries (See, for example, Unit 3 of the Excellence in Writing program: Retelling Narrative Stories) one to three paragraphs in length

- Paragraph-long descriptions of the author's use of particular literary devices, such as alliteration or imagery
- Paragraph-length descriptions of story characters or setting

Logic Level Writing Assignments:

- Key thought outline summaries as above (three to five paragraphs in length)
- Critiques as per Unit 9 of the Excellence in Writing program
- Page-long answers to questions from the Socratic List
- Simple essays on the significance of climactic moments to the story's theme
- Essays arguing for a particular climactic moment, demonstrating how it resolves a particular story conflict
- Essays identifying and arguing for a specific protagonist. (Depending upon the story, this can be harder than it sounds.)

Rhetoric Level Writing Assignments:

- Two to three page discussions of theme in which students are required to support their assertions with specific passages from the text that demonstrate their thesis, thereby proving that their reading of the story is tenable. For example:
    - I. Introduction: One theme of (name of book here) is (such and such theme).
    - II. The author uses (such and such elements) to illustrate his theme.
    - III. Based upon (such and such evidence) the author's perspective on this theme is (thus and so).
- Two to three page discussions of the author's use of literary devices and how they related to other aspects of the story such as characters, setting, and theme.
- "Compare and contrast" exercises dealing with the characters in a particular work.
- Persuasive essays arguing for a particular story protagonist or for the importance of a single conflict to the overall thematic ideas of the story.

Advanced rhetoric students ought to learn to write a literary research paper in which students research several "readings" of a classic story and present their analytical findings, arguing for one reading over and above another. These should include copious quotations and documentation.

The Story Chart

As has been demonstrated, the story chart can become a valuable source of notes and ideas when it comes time to write. The blank chart on the following page may be photocopied or modified to meet the needs of your classroom. In particular, each element of fiction identified on the chart might warrant more space as the student becomes more proficient at thinking about literature. As long as the spatial structure of the diagram is kept in mind as a guide, it is often helpful to older students to use blank sheets for note-taking in class discussions. At the high school level, for example, a student may take a page or two of notes for each element of fiction: Plot, Conflict, Setting, Character and Theme.

______________________________: Story Chart

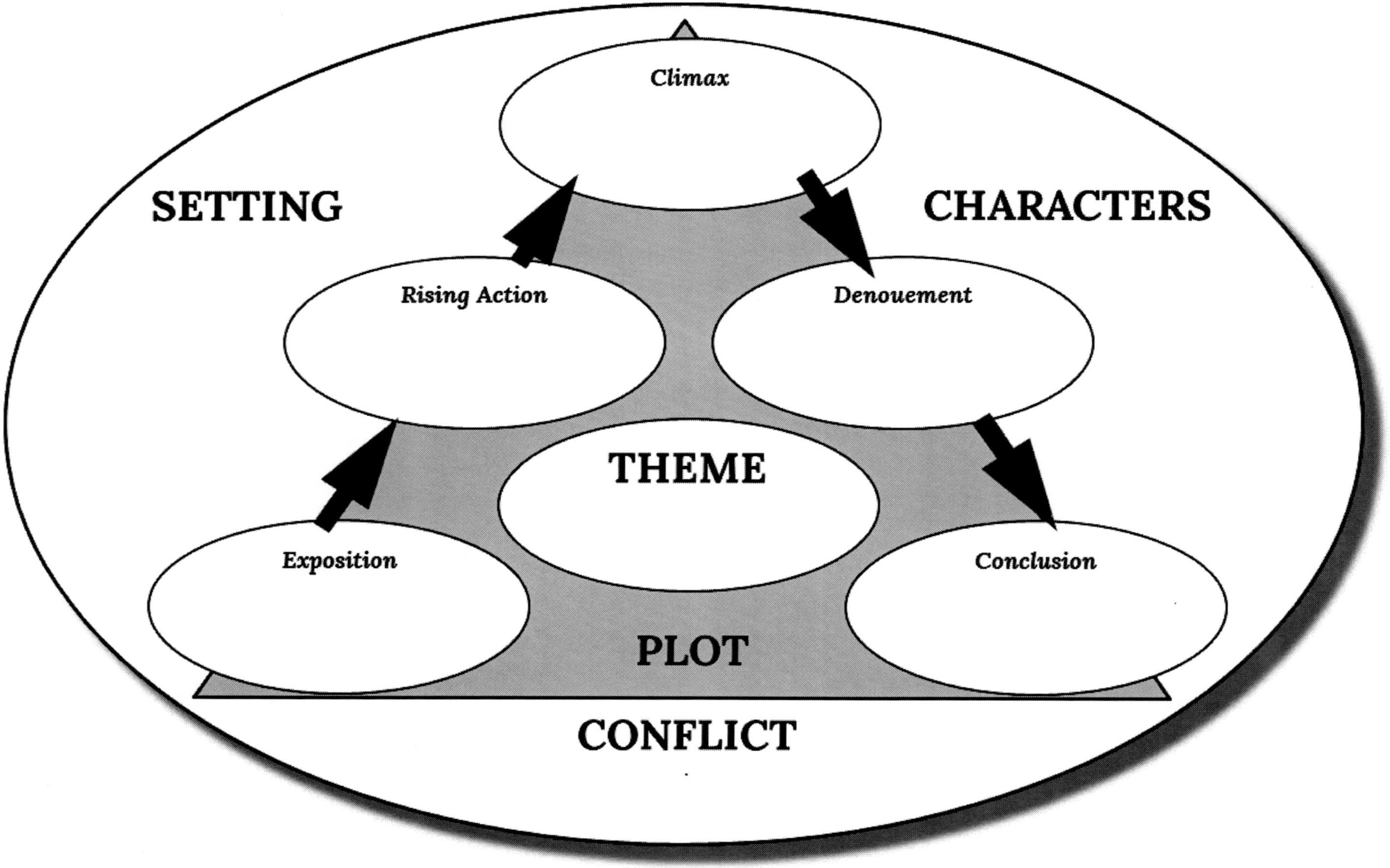
Climax
SETTING
CHARACTERS
Rising Action
Denouement
THEME
Exposition
Conclusion
PLOT
CONFLICT

SECTION 9: APPENDICES

APPENDIX A: THE SOCRATIC LIST

Questions About Setting

1. Where does this story happen?

a. In what country or region does the story happen?

b. Does the story happen in the country or the city?

c. Does the story happen in one spot, or does the action unfold across a wide area?

d. What is the mood or atmosphere of the place where the story happens? Is it cheerful and sunny, or dark and bleak? What words, phrases, or descriptions does the author use to create this atmosphere?

e. What is the weather like in the story?

f. Do you long to climb into the pages of the book to live in its world, or does it repel you? Why?

g. Is the setting a real or imaginary place? If it is imaginary, is it subject to the same physical laws as our world?

h. Among what kinds of people is the story set? What is their economic class? How do they live? Are they hopeful? Downtrodden? Depressed? Why?

i. Is there anything symbolic or allegorical about the place where the story happens?

j. Is the setting of the story important because of historical events which may have taken place there? How does this help you understand the themes of the story?

2. When does this story happen?

a. On what day does the story happen? What time of day?

b. How long a period of time does the story cover? A few minutes? A single day? A whole lifetime?

c. In what season does the story take place?

d. Does the story happen in a particular year, era, or age of the world? What historical events may have just preceded the period of the story? Do these events help explain the actions of characters, the action of the story, or its mood? (For example, is the story set in the midst of the Industrial Revolution in England like some of Charles Dickens' works, or is it set in the Roaring Twenties in America like Fitzgerald's work?)

e. In what time of life for the main characters do the events occur? Are they children? Are they just passing into adulthood? Are they already grown up? How does setting the story in this particular time of the characters' lives affect the story?

f. In what intellectual period is the story set? What ideas were prevalent during this period? Does the author deal with these ideas through his characters? Do the characters respond to social rules and customs that are the result of these ideas? (Jane Austen's books, for example, were set in the early nineteenth century in England, when women were bound by social laws forbidding them from owning or inheriting property. Consequently, marriage to men of property was their only source of financial security. Without this knowledge, the dialogue in *Pride and Prejudice* and the action of *Emma* are unintelligible to the modern reader.)

Questions About Characters

3. Who is the story about? (These questions may be asked about the protagonist or any other character.)

a. Is the character a man or an animal?

b. How old is the character?

c. Is the character male or female?

d. What does the character look like (hair, eyes, height, build, etc.)?

e. Is the character sane or insane?

f. Is the character kind, gentle, stern, emotional, harsh, logical, rational, compassionate or exacting? Make up a list of adjectives that describe the protagonist. What words or actions on the character's part make you choose the adjectives you do?

g. Of what nationality is the character? Does he live in his native land or somewhere else?

h. What does the character do for a living? Is he a professional or a blue-collar worker? Is he wealthy or impoverished? Is he content with his lot in life, or does he long to improve himself, like Pip in *Great Expectations*?

i. Is the character educated? To what degree? How do you know?

j. What does the character say about himself to other people?

k. What do other characters think or say about him?

l. Is the character a member of any particular religious or social group? If so, what do you know about this group? What motivates this group? What do its members feel to be important?

m. What does the character think is the most important thing in life? How do you know this? Does the character say this out loud, or do his thoughts and actions give him away?

n. Do the character's priorities change over the course of the story? In what way? What causes this change? Is it a change for the better, or for the worse?

o. How does the personality of the character reflect the values of the society (or individual) that produced the story?

p. Is the character a type or archetype? Is he an "Everyman" with whom the reader is meant to identify? Are his struggles symbolic of human life?

q. Is the character a sympathetic character? Do you identify with him and hope he will succeed? Do you pity him? Do you scorn or despise his weakness in some way? Why?

4. Who else is the story about?

a. Is there a single character (or a group of characters) that opposes the protagonist in the story? In other words, is there an **antagonist**?

b. In what way is he antagonistic? What goal of the protagonist does he oppose?

c. What actions does he take to oppose the protagonist?

d. Is the antagonist out to do physical harm to the protagonist, violence to his reputation, his memory, his work, or his family? How do you know?

e. How does the author's description of the character inform you of his antagonism? Does he have any physical attributes or personality traits that mark him as antagonistic?

f. Why does he oppose the protagonist? Does he merely belong to a different social group? Does he see the world in slightly different ways? Or is he an evil villain, like Shakespeare's Iago?

g. Is he reprehensible, so that none would wish to be like him?

h. How do this character's words and actions affect those around him?

i. Does his presence corrupt?

j. Is he strangely attractive? Does he draw others into his wicked sensibilities, e.g., Wormwood in *The Screwtape Letters?* Does he seem somehow rational, justified, even righteous in his actions, e.g., Javert in *Les Miserables?*

k. Has the antagonist always opposed the protagonist? If not, what caused his opposition?

l. Does the author believe this character to be responsible for his own sinfulness, or does he believe him a product of a "negative environment"?

m. Is the antagonist evil by definition, or is he merely antagonistic to the protagonist by virtue of his vocation or duty?

n. What are the antagonist's surroundings (does he live next door to the dump like Bob Ewell in *To Kill a Mockingbird*)? Are they related to his character? Did the author put him there on purpose?

Questions About Conflict

5. What does the protagonist want? ***(May also be asked of other characters)***

a. Fill in the blank: This story is about the protagonist trying to ________.

b. Does he attempt to overcome something – a physical impediment or an emotional handicap?

c. Does he strive to overcome a physical obstacle outside of himself (an ocean, for example, like Christopher Columbus, or nature generally, like a Jack London character)?

d. Does the protagonist try to capture an object (*The Silver Chalice*)?

   i. Or a person (Agatha Christie's Hercule Poirot)?

   ii. Or a beast (St. George and the Dragon)?

   iii. Or a perfect world (Thomas More's *Utopia*)?

   iv. Or a mate (*Pride and Prejudice*)?

   v. Or freedom (Harriet Tubman)?

   vi. Or success (*Goodbye, Mr. Chips*)?

   vii. Or justice (Jean Valjean of *Les Miserables*)?

   viii. Or psychological peace (*The Brothers Karamazov*)?

   ix. Or contentment (Does he even know what he's looking for)?

e. Is the conflict an external one, having to do with circumstances in the protagonist's physical world, or is it an internal conflict, taking place in his mind and emotions?

f. Do his objectives or goals change throughout the story? How? Why?

6. Why can't he have it?

a. Do physical or geographical impediments stand in the character's way?

b. Does the character lack strength, mental acumen, or some other necessary ability?

c. Does he lack self-confidence, good health, or social connections?

d. Does the character's age, economic class, race, or sex stand in his way?

e. Is the character racing against time?

f. Are there people other than the main antagonist who represent an obstacle to the character's pursuit of his goal?

g. Is the conflict a Man vs. Man struggle?

h. Is the conflict a Man vs. Nature struggle?

i. Is the conflict a Man vs. God or Fate struggle?

j. Is the conflict a Man vs. Society struggle?
k. Is the conflict a Man vs. Himself struggle?

7. What other problems are there in the story?

a. Are there other things in the story (people, responsibilities, etc.) that distract the characters from their main goals?
b. Do characters' actions provoke further conflict or unrest in the story?
c. Is the protagonist involved in more than one important conflict in the story (Scout vs. Boo Radley and Bob Ewell in *To Kill a Mockingbird*, for example)?
d. Are there other characters in the story who do not understand the protagonist's motives and ambitions?
e. Is there a conflict within the conflict (for example, the murderer turns out to be the detective's wife)?
f. Are there larger issues (a larger context or frame) in which conflict exists and forms a background for the story (a war setting, for example, as in Dickens' *Tale of Two Cities* or Tolstoy's *War and Peace*)?

Questions About Plot

8. What happens in the story?

a. What major events take place in the story as a result of the conflict?

b. How do the protagonist and the antagonist respond to the conflict initially? Do these actions provoke further conflict?

c. How do the interactions of the characters heighten the tension of the conflict that exists?

d. What external impulses heighten the conflict – weather, war, summer break, separation, sickness, etc.?

9. How is the main problem solved?

a. Does the protagonist achieve his object?

b. How are the protagonist's obstacles finally overcome?

c. Is the situation pleasantly resolved, or is it resolved in a terrible way?

d. What events form the highest point or climax of the story's tension? Are they circumstantial events, or emotional ones? Is the climax a spiritual or physical one?

e. Does the protagonist solve his own dilemma? Is it solved by some external source or third party? Is he helpless in the end to achieve his goal (like Frodo in *Lord of the Rings*), or does he triumph by virtue of his own efforts (Sherlock Holmes)?

f. Does the major conflict develop into a larger battle?

10. How does the story end?

a. After the climax of the story, did you wonder how it would end? How does it end? How are the "loose ends" tied up? Were all of your questions answered?

b. Were you satisfied with the resolution? If not, why not?

c. Do you believe the characters' responses to the cataclysmic events, or are they anti-climactic in some regard?

d. How does the solution of the conflict affect each individual character?

e. Does the ending or resolution of the story make any kind of judgments?

f. Does the resolution offer any particular perspective or understanding of the story's themes?

Questions About Theme

11. What does the protagonist learn?

a. Is the protagonist changed in his mind or heart by the events of the story?

b. Does he begin to act differently? In what way?

c. Is he ennobled?

d. Is he sacrificed in some way? (Was this a part of the climax or resolution?)

e. Does the main character explain to the reader his perspective regarding the events that have transpired?

f. Does he draw upon any motifs or symbols to deepen his explanation of these events?

12. What do the other characters learn?

a. Are other people in the story ennobled, changed, saved, improved or otherwise affected by the story's events?

b. Do they look at themselves differently at the end of the story?

c. Do they look at the protagonist differently?

d. Do they look at their surroundings or situations differently?

e. Do they re-examine their values and ideas?

13. What is the main idea of the story?

a. Does the story seem to deal with a universal theme like the ones listed in this syllabus?

b. How does the story answer the problem associated with that theme?

c. Does the story merely call the reader to observe a theme or human condition without providing any kind of resolution or solution?

d. What answer does the story seem to suggest for the question, "What is a good life?" How does the story present life, death, and love?

e. How does the author portray the human condition in order to provoke wonder?

Questions About Literary Devices

14. Does the author use the sounds of our language to create interest in his story?

Onomatopoeia –

a. Does the author use sound words to tell his story?

b. Does popcorn pop, soda pop fizz, and a horn bleat on any of the pages? Do any similar word sounds appear in the text?

Assonance –

c. Does the author use words in sequence or in close proximity which have the same internal vowel sounds?

Consonance –

d. Does the author use words in sequence or in close proximity that each end with the same consonant sound?

Alliteration –

e. Does the author use words in sequence or in close proximity that repeat the same initial consonant sound?

Rhyme –

f. Does the author end words or lines with the same final syllabic sounds to create a musical quality within the text?

15. Does the author use common words and phrases in uncommon ways?

Understatement –

a. Does the author intentionally represent things in language that is less strong than the situation or thing would necessarily warrant for purely rhetorical effect? (For example, in Ian Falconer's *Olivia*, the narrator mentions that Olivia learns to make sandcastles and gets "pretty good." The picture of a sand-cast model of the Empire State Building illustrates this. In *The Biggest Bear*, the author mentions the trappers from the zoo were "a little surprised" to see the boy in the trap with the bear.)

Hyperbole –

b. Does the author overstate or exaggerate things to make a point?

c. Do characters within the story make gross overstatements to drive home an issue or idea?

Cliché –

d. Does the author use figures of speech or expressions that are common and overused?

Oxymoron –

e. Does the author use sayings that are wiser than they appear at first glance?

f. Does the author juxtapose two normally contradictory words or ideas for the sake of making some wise insight? (a healing wound, a wise fool, a cruel kindness, icy hot)

16. Does the author use descriptions and comparisons to create pictures in the reader's mind?

Imagery –

a. Does the author create snapshots of images in the mind of the reader for the sake of enhancing meaning, creating setting or mood, or developing character?

b. Does the author rely upon similes, metaphors, or personification to convey his meaning more powerfully?

c. Does the author describe things by showing them to the reader via word pictures, rather than merely telling the reader about them?

Simile –

d. Does the author use the words "like" or "as" in making comparisons between two or more dissimilar things?

Personification –

e. Does the author represent inanimate objects as being lifelike or human?

f. Do things or creatures speak with human voices, expressing rational thoughts and ideas?

g. Do trees have arms and dance in the wind? Do birds sing sweetly in praise to God? Does the thunder bellow a warning note? Does the wind howl, "Go Hooome!" as it did in *Brave Irene*?

Metaphor –

h. Does the author make comparisons of dissimilar objects or things without the use of the words "like" or "as"?

i. Does the author call one thing or object another?

j. How does this help the author create a mood for the story?

k. How does it help him emphasize a theme?

l. Are any metaphors extended throughout the whole story, so that they sound like themes (symbols)?

17. Does the author use the characters and events in his story to communicate a theme that goes beyond them in some way?

Foreshadowing –

a. Does the author provide any clues early in the story of things to come in the plot?

b. Are there any hints of coming doom, disaster, excitement, blessing, or action?

c. Do characters utter statements that appear ironic in retrospect after the action occurs? Does the author let you in on the inner thoughts of his characters for the sake of underscoring potential disasters or events ahead in the story?

Irony –

d. When read literally, do the words of a character or narrator offer information that contradicts what you've already discovered to be true about a character's circumstances, character, or thoughts?

e. Do you know more about the character than the character himself does at any point in the story (*dramatic irony*)?

Allusion –

f. Does the author refer to other works of literature, historical events, works of art, or well-known ideas in his work?

g. Does the author's reference to other works, events, or ideas serve to underscore and enrich the reader's understanding of an event or character in the story?

Symbolism –

h. Does the author use any objects or ideas to refer to or embody a character quality or personal trait? For example, in *To Kill A Mockingbird*, Jem, Scout, Tom Robinson, and Boo are all "mockingbirds."

i. Does the author use any objects, persons, pictures, or things to represent an idea in the story? For example, darkness may be used to represent wickedness. Light may be used to represent truth and goodness. In the allegorical play, *Everyman*, the main character represents or symbolizes human nature. In the Christian tradition, the symbol of a dove often represents the person of the Holy Spirit.

Questions About Context

18. Who is the author?

a. What is the author's name?

b. Is the author male or female?

c. How old was the author when he wrote the story?

d. Was the author happy or unhappy? Friendly or reclusive?

e. What kinds of relationships did the author have? Did he have a family? Was he an orphan?

f. Did the author suffer any hardships in his life that might have made him think or feel a certain way about his subject?

g. Do the answers to these questions make themselves apparent in the author's story? In what ways?

19. Where did the author live?

a. In what country did the author live? In what city or state?

b. Did the author live in the city, or in the countryside?

c. Did the author live in poverty, or comfort?

d. Do the answers to these questions make themselves apparent in the author's story? In what ways?

20. When did the author live?

a. In what year was the author born? When did he die?

b. What events took place in the world during the author's lifetime? Did the author know about them? Was he involved in them?

c. Does the author refer to the events of his lifetime in his story?

d. Do the answers to these questions make themselves apparent in the author's story? In what ways?

21. What did the author believe?

a. Was the author a believer in a particular religion?

b. Was the author a member of a certain political party or other organization?

c. Was the author associated with a particular social cause or movement? (Examples include temperance, abolitionism, women's suffrage, civil rights, Puritanism, etc.)

d. Was the author associated with a particular intellectual school or mode of literature? (examples include Romanticism, Transcendentalism, Existentialism, Naturalism, Realism, Postmodernism, etc.)

e. Do the answers to these questions make themselves apparent in the author's story? In what ways?

f. Was the author's worldview in any way threatened by new philosophies, scientific discoveries, or personal circumstances? Was this conflict reflected in his stories?

APPENDIX B:
READING LISTS

Here are some of the books we love. This list is by no means exhaustive, of course. We are firmly convinced, in fact, that there is no such thing as an exhaustive list of good books! You will find great pleasure, if you have not already, in building a reading list of your own. To that end, we direct your attention to the booklist resources listed in this syllabus.

If you are new to book-gathering and would benefit from knowing where to start, here are some suggestions.

Stories for Young Children

Aardema, Verna – *Why Mosquitoes Buzz in People's Ears*

A disturbance in the forest causes an untimely death for one of Mrs. Owl's owlets. Blame shifting and false witness chase a rabbit trail of disaster back to the creature whose foolishness was the real cause of the tragedy. Repetition enchants the children.

Ackerman, Karen – *Song and Dance Man*

Grandpa used to be a vaudeville man. Enjoy his command attic performance with his grandchildren.

Azarian, Mary and Jacqueline Briggs Martin – *Snowflake Bentley*

A true story of William Bentley, the first man to study snowflakes and capture their images with photography, this story illustrates the rewards of perseverance, and patience in the pursuit of personal dreams.

Bemelmans, Ludwig – *Madeline*

"In an old house in Paris that was covered with vines…" lived Madeline. Join Madeline and her boarding school buddies as they discover the treasures of Paris and trouble their nervous headmistress, Miss Clavel.

Bishop, Claire H. – *Five Chinese Brothers*

Disobedience has drastic consequences for a tyke in this tall tale.

Brett, Jan – *The Mitten*

When a little boy receives new white mittens from his grandmother, he is encouraged not to lose them in the snow. Inevitably, his carelessness overtakes him. In his absence the lost mitten becomes home to more than his hand!

Brown, Marcia – *Stone Soup*

When stingy townsfolk refuse hospitality to some hungry soldiers, the clever men persuade them to share some stone soup with them.

Brown, Margaret Wise – *Goodnight Moon*

In child's voice, the text tells the tale of night-time leave-takings from dearly loved things.

Brown, Margaret Wise –*Little Fur Family*

"There was a little fur family, warm as toast, smaller than most…" So begins this small tale about a day in the life of a small bear.

Brown, Margaret Wise – *The Runaway Bunny*

A little bunny wants to run away, but his wise mother bunny deters him with her loving determination to seek him out regardless of his ventures.

Burton, Virginia – *Mike Mulligan and His Steam Shovel*

When newer and fancier diggers replace the old steam shovels, Mike stubbornly refuses to replace his own, dear steam shovel, Mary Anne. Searching for work, he vows she can still dig more in a day than a passel of men can dig in a week. Learn the inherent value friendship lends to cast off things.

Cohen, Barbara – *The Canterbury Tales, retold*

A group of medieval travelers on pilgrimage agree to entertain one another with stories of wit and wisdom on their trip to and from the shrine of St. Thomas Becket, with the best tale winning its teller a free meal upon their return. This beautifully illustrated re-telling of a few of Chaucer's famous tales is written in the spirit of Chaucer's original work. ("The General Prologue," "The Wife of Bath," and "The Pardoner's Tale")

Cooney, Barbara – *Chanticleer and the Fox*

A retelling of Geoffrey Chaucer's "Nun's Priest's Tale" from his *Canterbury Tales*, a vain rooster and a cunning fox match wits. This beast fable contains a moral lesson about pride and vanity. It works beautifully to introduce older students to its more difficult counterpart, Chaucer's original version.

Cooney, Barbara – *Miss Rumphius*

"Before you are old you must do something to make the world more beautiful." So says little Miss Rumphius's grandfather. After climbing the highest mountains and strolling on the farthest shores to survey nature's grandeur, an aging Miss Rumphius makes her own contribution to the world's beauty in her home town.

Dr. Seuss – *Horton Hears a Who*

Horton the elephant is hearing things! At least that is what his neighbors believe. In fact, Horton's big ears are picking up the cries of the Whos, minute creatures that live on a floating speck of dust. Horton, who appoints himself protector of the little universe, becomes a mouthpiece for the mute and a voice for the oppressed, proclaiming: "A person's a person no matter how small!"

Duvoisin, Roger – *Petunia*

When the sophomoric goose Petunia finds a book and pretends to be able to read it, she causes no end of trouble for herself and her animal friends. Posers never prosper!

Eastman, Philip D. – *Are You My Mother?*

A newly hatched nestling searches for his mother in unusual places.

Falconer, Ian – *Olivia*

Art driven, this simple story excels in characterization. Words and pictures combine to effect irony through understatement. Follow precocious, style conscious, energetic Olivia through a typical day of activity.

Flack, Marjorie and Kurt Wiese – *The Story About Ping*

While diving for a fish one evening, the little duckling Ping misses the boatman's call to come aboard. Fearing retribution, he hides in the reeds along the bank and is left behind. Alone for the first time on the river, Ping encounters a host of greater terrors in the other animals and boatmen.

Fox, Mem – *Wilfred Gordon McDonald Partridge*

Wilfred, who lives next to an old folks' home, is puzzled when he hears that his best friend, Mrs. Delacourt, has lost her memory. Join him on his quest to restore it.

Freeman, Don – *Dandelion*

When Dandelion the lion makes a dandy of himself for a party with the gang, his dearest friends fail to recognize him. A lesson in being oneself.

Gramatky, Haardie – *Little Toot*

Little Toot is tugboat in training. Frolicking irresponsibly in the surf, he becomes a nuisance to others, endangering many lives until discipline shames him, and he rises to the occasion to save the day.

Hall, Donald and Barbara Cooney – *Ox-Cart Man*

Follow a self-sufficient farm family through a year of seasons.

Hoban, Russell and Lillian – *A Bargain for Frances*

Young Frances learns a valuable lesson in friendship and honesty when her sometime friend and oft-time foe cheats her out of some money she had been saving for a china tea set "with pictures all in blue."

Hoban, Russell and Lillian – *Bedtime for Frances*

Little Frances can't sleep. Alert and perpetually distracted by her fertile imagination, she pesters her parents until her father reminds her of the consequences for disobedience.

Hoban, Russell and Lillian – *Bread and Jam for Frances*

Another Frances delight! This time Frances, a bread and jam girl, realizes that variety truly is the spice of life.

Hoberman, Mary Ann – *A House is A House For Me*

Rhyming throughout, this book is an exploration of metaphor. The musical cadences it creates and the interesting perspective the comparisons provide make children giggle with delight.

Hodges, Margaret – *Saint George and the Dragon*

Visit the medieval period with this beautifully retold and handsomely illustrated legend of an English Christian crusader who slew a dragon that was menacing a foreign village.

Krauss, Ruth – *The Carrot Seed*

When a little boy plants a carrot seed, his entire family contends that it won't come up! Even so, he waters and cares for the seed, believing that his efforts will be rewarded. A lesson in faith.

Leaf, Munro – *The Story of Ferdinand*

Unlike other bulls his age, Ferdinand is passive and placid by nature. When an encounter with a bee makes him snort and stomp, bull fighters mistake him for a fierce fighter and whisk him off to the bullring in Madrid.

Lionni, Leo – *The Biggest House in the World*

When a small snail declares to his father his desire to have the biggest house in the world, his father enlightens him with a moral tale about a snail who experiences the consequences of building too big.

MacLachlan, Patricia – *All the Places to Love*

A young boy poetically depicts the ties that bind a family to a plot of ground for generations.

McCloskey, Robert – *Blueberries for Sal*

When little Sal and her mother go berry picking on Blueberry Hill, they find that humans are not the only ones who store fruit for winter!

McCloskey, Robert – *Make Way for Ducklings*

Once Mr. and Mrs. Mallard have found the perfect spot for laying their eggs, they settle in for the imminent arrival of Jack, Kack, Lack, Mack, Nack, Oack, Pack, and Quack! Also by McCloskey: *Time of Wonder*, *Lentil*, *One Morning in Maine.*

Milne, A.A. and E.H. Shepard – *Winnie-the-Pooh*

Join Christopher Robin and his animal friends for adventures in the Hundred-Acre-Wood in these heartwarming stories.

Ness, Evaline – *Sam, Bangs & Moonshine*

Sam is a motherless girl whose fantastic imagination keeps her company during her fisherman father's long absences. When her fantasies endanger the lives of her favorite cat and her neighbor friend Thomas, however, she discovers the importance of telling the truth.

Pfister, Marcus – *The Rainbow Fish*

The rainbow fish bedazzles all the fish in his part of the sea with his brilliant and colorful scales. Although the other fish beg him to share some of his beauty, he refuses until loneliness changes his mind.

Piper, Watty – *The Little Engine That Could*

When the train carrying food and toys to the children of a valley town breaks down, the littlest engine of all gladly assumes the big responsibility of getting it all there.

Polacco, Patricia – *Thunder Cake*

A narrator recalls the day her grandmother helps her to overcome her fear of thunder. Also by Polacco: *The Keeping Quilt*, *Thank You Mr. Falker*, *The Bee Tree*, *Babushka Baba Yaga*, *My Rotten Redheaded Older Brother, Pink and Say, Chicken Sunday,* and *The Butterfly.*

Potter, Beatrix – *The Tale of Peter Rabbit*

After a close scrape in Farmer McGregor's garden, disobedient Peter learns the value of heeding his mother's voice.

Priceman, Marjorie – *How to Make an Apple Pie and See the World*

With the local grocery closed for the day, a young girl travels the world to obtain key ingredients for her apple pie, inviting the international friends she meets along the way to share in the final product.

Rylant, Cynthia – *Henry and Mudge*

This series of early readers showcases the growing affection between a boy and his dog – in this case a big, sloppy beast named Mudge.

Rylant, Cynthia – *The Relatives Came*

When the relatives come, home seems unfamiliar, filled with strange smells, sounds, and people! The strangeness, however, is as welcome as they are, and a stranger silence fills the house when they depart.

Sendak, Maurice – *Where the Wild Things Are*

When disobedient Max is sent to his room without his supper, he takes an imaginary journey to join other monsters like himself for a wild romp!

Slobodkina, Esphyr – *Caps for Sale*

A cap peddler awakes from an afternoon nap to find his goods nabbed by some monkeys up to their usual business.

Steig, William – *Amos & Boris*

When kindly whale Boris saves the little mouse Amos from drowning, he hardly expects to be repaid in kind, but he discovers that no creature is too small to offer great service to a friend in need.

Steig, William – *Brave Irene*

With her seamstress mother sick in bed, Irene must brave the gathering storm to deliver the ball dress to the duchess in time for the ball.

Stewart, Sarah and David Small – *The Gardener*

Set in the Great Depression, a young farm girl is sent to the city to work in her uncle's bakery. There, her tenacious hope and joy root and grow in everyone she touches. Also by the author: *The Library* and *The Friend.*

Tiller, Ruth – *Cinnamon, Mint and Mothballs: A Visit to Grandmother's House*

Full of sensory language and poetic imagery, a young girl remembers a visit to her grandmother's house.

Turkle, Brinton – *Thy Friend, Obadiah*

When Obadiah frees a gull from some wire, he gains a faithful friend.

Van Allsburg, Chris – *The Polar Express*

On Christmas Eve, a boy with doubts about Santa Claus takes a train trip to the North Pole and discovers the value of childlike faith. Also by Van Allsburg: *The Wreck of the Zephyr, Jumanji, The Wretched Stone.*

Waber, Bernard – *You Look Ridiculous Said the Rhinoceros to the Hippopotamus*

Idle words send an unfortunate hippo on a journey of self-discovery.

Ward, Lynd – *The Biggest Bear*

When little Johnny Orchard, tired of losing face, declares he is going to hunt a bear to keep pace with the neighbors, he finds a friend instead. As his bear grows, Johnny must face a world of adult responsibilities. This coming of age story bears much resemblance to *The Yearling*, yet preserves a happy ending appropriate for its audience.

Yolen, Jane – *All Those Secrets of the World*

Janie cries when her daddy must go to war, but she discovers that distance is a really a matter of perspective.

Yolen, Jane – *Owl Moon*

A sensory treat, this story of a small child gone owling with her father captures a child's wonder of the world. More poem than story, this is a wonderful tool for teaching imagery, similes, metaphors, and sensory language.

Ziefert, Harriet – *A New Coat for Anna*

Anna needs a new coat, but war makes provisions difficult to find. Follow the process her mother takes in bartering to obtain the prized possession, and learn with Anna patience, appreciation, and a mother's sacrificial love.

Zolotow, Charlotte – *Big Sister and Little Sister*

Little sisters often become annoyed by their protective elder siblings. Yet, when one little sister secrets herself in a field of wildflowers, she finds her older sister's constant attentions stem from love.

Zolotow, Charlotte – *Something is Going to Happen*

Experience the breathless anticipation and wonder of the first snow of the year through the pages of Charlotte Zolotow's book.

Juvenile Fiction

Alcott, Louisa May – *Little Women*

Loosely based upon the life of the author, this narrative recounts the ambitions and struggles of the four March sisters growing up in Civil War era New England. Each sister struggles to be good, but is afflicted with some moral defect. Only kind Beth is content and good. When afflicted with scarlet fever she contracts while doing an act of charity, Beth suffers terribly, causing introspective Jo to ponder the goodness of God and wrestle with her own ambitions. Other books by Alcott include *Little Men* and *Jo's Boys*.

Alexander, Lloyd – *The Book of Three*

Assistant Pig-Keeper Taran, frustrated with his humdrum existence in Caer Dallben, yearns for a warrior's life like his hero, Prince Gwydion. His wish comes all too true as he faces the evil leader who threatens the peace of Prydain: the Horned King. The first in a series of five books which culminates in Newbery Award-winning *The High King.*

Atwater, Richard and Florence – *Mr. Popper's Penguins*

When work slows for the winter, housepainter Mr. Popper finds it difficult to keep up with the expenses of his growing family. Receiving an unexpected gift of penguins from a friend, he and his family create a stage act to become a household name in entertainment and eliminate financial worries for good!

Babbitt, Natalie – *Tuck Everlasting*

Young Winnie encounters the Tucks, an unusual family who claim to have found the fountain of youth. Her relationship with them draws her into a dangerous adventure and changes her perspective about ordinary life.

Banks, Lynne Reid – *The Indian in the Cupboard* (series)

After placing his plastic, model Indian in an old cupboard he received for his birthday, a little boy finds his toy has come alive! The magical properties of his cupboard become evident when he changes other toys into living creatures as well. The novelty of this magic wears thin, however, as the boy discovers the monolithic responsibility of a creator.

Bibee, John – *The Magic Bicycle*

When John Kramar finds an old, rusty Spirit Flyer bicycle, he never suspects it to be magical. First, the bike helps him save a neighbor's barn from burning. Then it brings him into conflict with forces that want to destroy it. Join John on his fantastic ride to learn about the Magic in the bicycle and save his town.

Brink, Carol Ryrie – *Caddie Woodlawn*

Child of an American pioneer family, Caddie is a tomboy extraordinaire! Growing up running with her brothers in the woods around their Wisconsin homestead, Caddie's adventures depict nineteenth century frontier life during the American Civil War.

Burgess, Alan – *The Small Woman*

This biography chronicles the life of Gladys Aylward, a British Christian missionary to China, who led more than 100 children over the mountains to safety in 1938 during the Japanese invasion of China.

Burnett, Frances Hodgson – *The Secret Garden*

Hodgson's characterization of a sour British girl who is orphaned in Africa and packed home to live with her absent and dour uncle in his gloomy castle on a moor continues to enchant readers. The quiet joy of country life, combined with the mysterious dual discovery of both a sickly cousin and a forgotten, walled garden, provide our orphan castoff with opportunities to see beyond herself. Learning the joy of giving, she embraces life, touching off an epidemic of miraculous resurrections and restorations of the heart! Other books by Burnett include *A Little Princess* and *Little Lord Fauntleroy.*

Burnford, Sheila – *The Incredible Journey*

Three lost pets find their way across an incredible distance to be reunited with their lost family.

Burroughs, Edgar Rice – *Tarzan*

Boys still devour these stories of the chest beating ape-man, raised by gorillas when his own family was slaughtered and grown to be lord of the jungle.

Cleary, Beverly – *Henry and Ribsy*

Henry has always wanted a dog, but he did not expect that keeping Ribsy out of trouble would prove a full-time job. Also by Cleary: *Henry and Beezus*, *Ramona the Pest*, *The Mouse and the Motorcycle*, *Runaway Ralph.*

Dalgliesh, Alice - *The Bears on Hemlock Mountain*

Short chapters make this a friendly book for a young reader. Follow a boy on an errand over the forested hill of his home to borrow a cast iron pot from his aunt. On the way, he will discover if there really are bears on Hemlock Mountain.

Dalgliesh, Alice – *The Courage of Sarah Noble*

Meet a daughter of the American Revolution. Orphaned and alone, she must make her way amid the terrors of the New England countryside in wartime.

Dahl, Roald – *Charlie and the Chocolate Factory*

When poor Charlie Bucket finds a golden ticket, he and his grandfather embark on a life-changing tour of Willy Wonka's Chocolate Factory. Also by Dahl: *Charlie and the Great Glass Elevator*, and *Danny, The Champion of the World.*

De Angeli, Marguerite – *A Door in the Wall*

His father at war and his mother at court, a young master of the house is left at home awaiting an escort to his new post as apprentice. An unidentified illness, however, strikes him down and leaves him lame. When the remaining servants fall prey to the Black Plague, the needy boy is cared for by a monk who teaches him how to overcome adversity.

Dixon, Franklin W. – *The Hardy Boys* series

Frank and Joe Hardy team up to solve countless mysteries in this series for young boys. The older books in the series are the best, as they are unaffected by twenty-first century political correctness.

Doyle, Arthur Conan – *The Adventures of Sherlock Holmes*

Famed Scotland Yard detective Sherlock Holmes solves a variety of murders and mysteries and always gets his man through "elementary" reasoning.

Edmonds, Walter – *The Matchlock Gun*

The heart-thumping story of a young boy who defends his mother and sister against an Indian raid during the American French and Indian War. A testimony to the importance of obedience.

Estes, Eleanor - *The Moffats*

These adventures of children in a single-parent family reinforce the providential nature of life. Also by Estes: *The Middle Moffat, Ginger Pye*, and *The Hundred Dresses.*

Field, Rachel – *Calico Bush*

In this work of historical fiction, thirteen-year-old Maggie, orphaned by her parents in the New World, finds herself forced into indentured servitude and must move with her new family to the wilds of Maine.

Fitzgerald, John D. – *The Great Brain*

These stories narrate the adventures of boy genius Tom D. Fitzgerald as related by his younger brother John, two boys growing up in Adenville, Utah, at the close of the nineteenth century. The first in a series of must read adventures!

Forbes, Esther – *Johnny Tremain*

Johnny is a talented but arrogant silver-smith's apprentice of Revolutionary era Boston whose life is turned upside-down when he injures his hand. In time he becomes a messenger boy on horseback for the Sons of Liberty and an eyewitness to the historic events surrounding the Revolution.

Fritz, Jean – *The Cabin Faced West*

In this story of early America, young Ann Hamilton and her family move West to stake a claim and carve a life out of the wilderness. Paced appropriately for early readers.

Gannett, Ruth S. – *My Father's Dragon*

Elmer Elevator journeys to far away Wild Island to rescue a dragon enslaved by island natives. This is an easy chapter book for young readers.

Gates, Doris – *Blue Willow*

Set in Depression Era California, a migrant family and their little girl, Janey Lark, long for a home and permanence.

George, Jean Craighead – *My Side of the Mountain*

A teenage boy leaves home to live a solitary life in the Catskill Mountain wilderness. Through his efforts to survive, he learns the value of independence and self-sufficiency.

Gilbreth, Frank and Ernestine Gilbreth Carey – *Cheaper By the Dozen*

Frank and Ernestine recollect their experiences growing up in a family of twelve. Their larger-than-life father and rock-steady mother provided them with all the warmth, love, and stability necessary to grow to maturity.

Gipson, Fred – *Old Yeller*

A stray dog finds a place as protector of a family in the wilds of Texas.

Grahame, Kenneth – *The Wind in the Willows*

Follow the rollicking adventures of Mr. Toad of Toad Hall and his most loyal, dear friends Badger, Mole, and Ratty. Rich with the sights and smells of the English countryside and replete with descriptions of prototypical picnics, the atmospheric qualities of this episodic narrative are in themselves enough to recommend it.

Grahame, Kenneth – *The Reluctant Dragon* (with pictures by E. H. Shepard)

Clear and imaginative, Grahame's main character is an intelligent boy who happens upon a dragon that refuses to be, well, dragonish. When legendary hero St. George comes to town, the dragon applies to the boy to intercede.

Gray, Elizabeth Janet – *Adam of the Road*

Adam loves his little dog almost as much as he loves his talented and gregarious father, a minstrel in medieval England. When separated from them both on a road trip, Adam is forced to use his wits and his talents to care for himself and regain his family.

Henry, Marguerite – *Misty of Chincoteague*

Two young residents of Assateague Island are determined to find and secure the Phantom, the mysterious and elusive wild horse of Chincoteague Island, for their own.

Holling, Holling C. – *Paddle-to-the-Sea*

Seemingly misplaced in the juvenile book list, this is a story of the travels of a small, hand-carved toy canoe, fearlessly manned by the wooden Indian carved into him. Though it is a picture book, the richly detailed text provides a wonderful backdrop for geography lessons. Also by Holling: *Seabird.*

Hunt, Irene – *Across Five Aprils*

Set in the Civil War era, a young boy experiences the the war that divides the nation when his brothers enlist with opposing sides. An extraordinarily well-told coming of age story.

Juster, Norton – *The Phantom Tollbooth*

When a bored youngster drives through a mysterious tollbooth that magically appears in his bedroom, he finds himself in Dictionopolis, an allegorical land full of surprises and life lessons.

Keene, Carolyn – *Nancy Drew* stories

Heroine Nancy Drew is the Sherlock in this mystery series for young girls. These are the counterparts to *Hardy Boys Mysteries* for boys. Look for the older ones; they are the best!

Keith, Harold – *Rifles for Watie*

In this coming-of-age Civil War drama, the main character, Jeff, goes undercover behind enemy lines, allowing him to see the war from the perspectives of both the north and the south. He discovers that there are men of principle on both sides of the battle; how will he choose between them?

Kipling, Rudyard – *The Jungle Book*

These seven unique short stories feature talking animals – some in the jungle, others in far north. Each teaches some character quality or principle. One teaches "jungle law," another the value of duty, still another the importance of courage. The riveting story of "Rikki-Tikki-Tavi," a faithful mongoose, is perhaps the best known of this book.

Konigsburg, E. L. – *From the Mixed-Up Files of Mrs. Basil E. Frankweiler*

Two runaways find shelter in New York's Metropolitan Museum of Art where they become gripped in an art mystery.

L'Engle, Madeleine – *A Wrinkle in Time* and series

The Wallace children, together with their friend Calvin, journey through a tesseract to find their missing father. Together they encounter strange forces of evil that threaten to prevent them from accomplishing their aims. Other books in this series include *A Wind In the Door*, *A Swiftly Tilting Planet*, and *Many Waters*.

Lamb, Charles and Mary – *Tales from Shakespeare*

Lamb's Tales are accessible narrative retellings of a few of Shakespeare's most celebrated plays. Clearly related, these stories introduce new readers to some of Shakespeare's greatest plots, laying the groundwork for deeper study of the original works of the master.

Lawson, Robert – *Rabbit Hill*

This challenging book is a vocabulary builder for young readers! Lawson's sensitive portrayal of a community of rabbits upset by the coming of new land owners is, in places, reminiscent of the *Brer Rabbit* stories of the South. Will the new folks be friendly to the local wildlife? Also by Lawson: *Ben and Me*, and *Mr. Revere and I.*

Leaf, Munro – *Wee Gillis*

Written by the author of the beloved children's book *Ferdinand*, this is the story of a Scottish boy born to a Lowlander and a Highlander, who must decide for himself with which clan to identify. Again, this story is an accessible read for early chapter book readers.

Lenski, Lois – *Strawberry Girl*

The story of a Florida Cracker girl and her childhood on a farm. A Newbery Award winner.

Lewis, C. S. – *The Chronicles of Narnia*

This enchanting allegorical series follows four children on their magical adventures to the land of Narnia, where good and evil battle for supremacy. There they learn important truths about themselves and become acquainted with Aslan, Narnia's good and rightful king.

Lindgren, Astrid – *Pippi Longstocking*

This series follows the delightful antics of the strongest girl in the world – independent, high spirited, and in charge of things in her seafaring father's absence.

MacDonald, George – *The Princess and the Goblin*

A young miner, Curdie, overhears the goblins' plan to invade the kingdom and unseat the king; with the help of Princess Irene and her great-great-grandmother, he must stop them. This fantasy/fairy tale extols the virtues of faith, honesty, courage, and honor. Its author was profoundly influential on C.S. Lewis. Also by MacDonald: *The Princess and Curdie*, *At the Back of the North Wind*, and *The Light Princess*.

MacLachlan, Patricia – *Sarah, Plain and Tall*

A mail-order bride becomes the lynchpin of her new Midwestern plains family. Also by this author, *Skylark*.

McSwigan, Marie – *Snow Treasure*

Set in World War II, the brave children of a Norwegian village help to secret the contents of the national treasury out of the country on their sleds in order to keep it from their German oppressors. Based on a true story.

Merrill, Jean – *The Pushcart War*

This satirical account of a feud between New York pushcart operators and the semi-trucks that congest the city suggests with humor the conflict of interest that lies at the heart of every war.

Milne, A. A. – *Winnie the Pooh*

Written for Milne's son Christopher, these tender and imaginative stories encompass the hilarious journeys and madcap mishaps of the residents of the Hundred Acre Wood. After meeting Pooh, Piglet, Owl, Tigger, Eeyore, Rabbit, Kanga, and Roo, your child will never be the same.

Montgomery, L. M. – *Anne of Green Gables* (series)

Precocious orphan Anne with an "e" is taken in by Marilla and Matthew, who discover in their act of charity that they need her more than they knew.

Morey, Walt – *Gentle Ben*

Mark's attachment to a brown bear held in captivity and abused by a local neighbor is jeopardized when well-meaning neighbors discover the situation.

Mowat, Farley – *Owls in the Family*

A hilarious series of anecdotes centering upon the addition of two owlets, Wol and Weeps, to young Billy's virtual zoo of family pets. Also by Mowat: *Never Cry Wolf, The Dog Who Wouldn't Be, The Snow Walker,* and *A Whale for the Killing.*

Neimark, Anne E. – *Touch of Light: The Story of Louis Braille*

When his eye is punctured during childhood, Louis goes blind. Hindered but not thwarted, Louis succeeds in finding a way to read and shares this with others with impaired vision.

Nesbit, Edith – *The Enchanted Castle*

Some displaced children stumble upon a magical castle and a not so magical princess during one of their holidays. Also by Nesbit: *Five Children and It*, The Railway Children, and The Treasure Seekers.

O'Brien, Robert – *Mrs. Frisby and the Rats of NIMH*

When Mrs. Frisby's son comes down with pneumonia just before spring plowing, she is unable to evacuate her field home. She applies to the rats of NIMH for help. These laboratory rats, super-intelligent from their use in a scientific experiment, have escaped from captivity and established an advanced community in the farmer's rose bush. Together with Mrs. Frisby, they pit their intellects against their greatest common foe, man.

O'Dell, Scott – *Island of the Blue Dolphins*

When a young girl is unintentionally abandoned on an island during one of her tribe's occasional outings, she is forced to learn survival skills. Also by O'Dell: the sequel *Zia, Sarah Bishop, Streams to the River, River to the Sea, The King's Fifth,* and *The Black Pearl.*

Pyle, Howard – *Otto of the Silver Hand*

Pyle tells the story of Otto, a child caught in the crossfire of violence and malice between two robber barons, his father, and a neighbor, during the medieval period. Also by Pyle: *The Story of Sir Lancelot and His Companions*, *Some Merry Adventures of Robin Hood*, and *The Story of King Arthur and His Knights.*

Rackham, Arthur, and C. S. Evans – *Cinderella*

Ella is a well-born girl, bereft of her mother, and emotionally abandoned by her father to the abuse of her new step-mother and step-sisters. Her gentleness and submissive nature are rewarded by the favor and protection of a fairy godmother, who aids her in her mother's absence.

Rawls, Wilson – *Where the Red Fern Grows*

Billy saves and buys two coonhounds for a song; they become priceless, loyal defenders of the family. A boy's ritc of passage, this book is a tale of love and responsibility.

Robinson, Barbara – *The Best Christmas Pageant Ever*

Meet the Herdman family. They are ornery, raucous, and plentiful, and they have come to take over the annual church Christmas pageant. Hark, the herald Herdmans sing! Will the community survive them? Also by Robinson: *The Best School Year Ever.*

Selden, George – *The Cricket in Times Square*

A misplaced cricket finds himself in the Times Square subway station. There he befriends Mario, a young boy whose family owns a newspaper stand; Tucker, a mouse; and Harry, a cat. Together the four work to save the family newsstand from bankruptcy.

Sewall, Marcia – *The Pilgrims of Plimoth*

This first-person narration recounts the experiences of the New England Puritans from their own point of view.

Sewell, Anna – *Black Beauty*

Black Beauty, a horse, tells his life story in episodic chapters.

Speare, Elizabeth George – *The Bronze Bow*

This piece of historical fiction explores the nature and effects of bitterness and hatred and the miraculous healing of forgiveness. A Newbery winner, it is a tender account of a wounded child's journey to maturity. Other books by Speare: *The Sign of the Beaver*, *The Witch of Blackbird Pond* (also a Newbery winner), and *Calico Captive*.

Sperry, Armstrong – *Call It Courage*

Author of some of the most gripping adventure stories ever written, Sperry tells the story of a young boy and his unflinching fight with fear. Also by Sperry: *The Black Falcon*, *All Sails Set: A Romance of the Flying Cloud*, and *Thunder Country.*

Spyri, Johanna – *Heidi*

The uplifting story of an orphan girl and the profound influence of her buoyant spirit and unconditional love upon her grandfather.

Sterling, Dorothy – *Freedom Train*

The moving true story of Harriet Tubman, an escaped slave who returned to the South repeatedly to secret more than 300 slaves to freedom using the Underground Railroad.

Taylor, Mildred - *Roll of Thunder, Hear My Cry*

A good look at the realities of racial tension in 1940's Mississippi, this Newbery Award winning book tells the story of the Logans, who boycott a local store to protest racial violence and incur the wrath of their neighbors.

Tolkien, J.R.R. – *The Hobbit*

Bilbo Baggins is a hobbit – a wee one, content to live out his life in the obscurity of his humble home in the Shire. When the great wizard Gandalf raps on his door, however, he finds himself pushed into the wilds and an adventure of epic proportions. Dragons and goblins and giants and darkness assail him in his quest to burgle the avaricious and thieving dragon of the mountain in order to return his horde to the dwarves, who claim rightful ownership of the loot. Bilbo acquires a magical ring along the way, which aids him in his journey and resurfaces in Tolkien's more mature trilogy *The Lord of the Rings*, written for older readers.

Twain, Mark – *The Adventures of Tom Sawyer*

Precocious Tom Sawyer is peerless when it comes to wit and humor. Twain paints a nostalgic picture of the vicissitudes of boyhood in this timeless classic. Also by Twain: *Huckleberry Finn.*

Warner, Gertrude C. – *The Boxcar Children*

A family of orphaned children determine to stay together and out of the custody of governmental officials who might divvy them out to various family members. Finding shelter in an abandoned boxcar, the elder children care for the younger.

White, E. B. – *Charlotte's Web*

Charlotte is an astounding arachnid! When she appears one morning in the door of Wilbur's lonely barn, the little pig's life is forever changed. Through Charlotte, the runt of the litter discovers personal value, potential, and the nature of true friendship.

White, E. B. – *The Trumpet of the Swan*

When a cygnet is born without a voice, his father determines to rectify the situation. Robbing a local music store, he obtains a trumpet to be his son's voice. Mastering this device, the intelligent bird resolves to earn money as an entertainer to reimburse the music store owner.

Wiggin, Kate Douglas – *Rebecca of Sunnybrook Farm*

Discover the classic Mark Twain called the best story of American literature. Rebecca, sent from home to live with her two aunts, charms readers with her imagination and high spirits. Overcoming adversity, she grows to become an independent woman.

Wilder, Laura Ingalls - *Little House on the Prairie* series

Laura Ingalls Wilder revisits her childhood on the frontier in this beloved series of children's classics.

Wyss, Johann David – *Swiss Family Robinson*

A shipwrecked family works together to survive on a desert island until help can arrive.

High School Fiction

Adams, Richard – *Watership Down*

Spurred on by the prophetic visions of their companion Fiver, Hazel, Bigwig, and the other rabbits flee their comfortable warren to avoid an unnamed, impending destruction. Their subsequent journey to find a new home explores the themes of leadership, courage, and loyalty – and raises thoughtful questions about the nature of a good society. A heart-thumping, provocative adventure about so much more than bunnies.

Austen, Jane – *Pride and Prejudice*

Elizabeth lives in a period in which a girl's only hope was to marry well. Unable to inherit from fathers and husbands, women were forced to hope in the kindness of their male relations for subsistence. Initially put off by social prejudices, proud Mr. Darcy ultimately finds himself drawn to Miss Bennett's straightforward honesty and simple wisdom. Licking her own wounded pride, she rejects his advances. Yet when a wandering eye draws her younger sister into a promiscuous affair, Elizabeth must rely on Darcy's kindness to make matters right. Not only a period romance, but also a social satire, this timeless classic rewards rereading. Also by Austen: *Sense and Sensibility*, *Emma*, *Persuasion*, and *Northanger Abbey.*

Beowulf

This early English epic recounts the exploits of Norse hero Beowulf. First a warrior, he fights against the vicious and murderous monster Grendel; later a king, he confronts a fiery dragon. With its syncretistic Christian and pagan elements, Beowulf explores the role of king and warrior in fifth- and sixth-century Scandinavia.

Bradbury, Ray – *The Martian Chronicles*

Post-apocalyptic science fiction about the destruction of earth through nuclear explosion and the colonization of Mars, this series of short stories were initially published serially for magazines.

Bronte, Charlotte – *Jane Eyre*

Orphaned Jane is shipped off to live in an intolerably harsh asylum for castoff girls; she longs for love. The darkness of her life, however, does not quench her gentle spirit, but rather produces character, perseverance, and love.

Cather, Willa – *My Antonia*

Set in the early American West, an immigrant family must make a living in an inhospitable terrain.

Chaucer, Geoffrey – *The Canterbury Tales*

Pilgrims off to see the shrine of St. Thomas a Becket agree to entertain one another with stories on their journey and to reward the narrator of the best story with a free meal upon their return. In this way, the tales are born. Their subjects and themes betray the character and nature of their tellers, giving the reader a glimpse into the the personalities of the Middle Ages and likewise demonstrating the timeless nature of man. This literary gem is a relic of its period for the historian and etymologist as it represents the first literary work ever written in the English vernacular. It is well-paired with Barbara Cohen's adaptation, which is beautifully illustrated by Trina Schart Hyman.

Conrad, Joseph – *Heart of Darkness*

A profound study of the sinfulness of man, this story involves the protagonist Marlowe's journey into imperial Britain's outposts in the African jungle. Expecting to find Britain's benevolent rule civilizing savages, he is dismayed to discover British brutality instead, enslaving the natives and using them for commercial gain.

Cooper, James Fenimore – *The Last of the Mohicans*

The first great American novel, Cooper's sweeping epic portrays the clash of civilizations that took place during the 1750's French and Indian War in vivid and gripping detail. "Noble Savages" confront savage Europeans, and the hero must choose between the two civilizations.

Costain, Thomas – *The Silver Chalice*

Based on legends of the years following Jesus's crucifixion, this novel describes the life and travels of Basil, the artisan who fashioned the silver chalice that held the sacred cup from which Jesus drank at the Last Supper.

Crane, Stephen – *The Red Badge of Courage*

In this masterpiece of literary realism and naturalism, journalist Stephen Crane imagines the effects of the American Civil War on the idealism of a young enlisted man, and in so doing contemplates the legitimacy of universal truth itself. Also by Crane: *The Blue Hotel* and *The Open Boat.*

D'Orczy, Baroness – *The Scarlet Pimpernel*

Set during the French Revolution, this story follows the movements of a mysterious hero, who secrets aristocrats and other targets of the revolutionaries out of the country. His infamous exploits become the pulp of gossip in the English social circles frequented by newly married Marguerite, who wishes she had married the mysterious fellow instead of her own, dull spouse.

Dante – *The Divine Comedy*

The first literary work ever to be written in the Italian vernacular, Dante's *Comedy,* a work in three books, narrates the author's imaginative and enlightening journey through the regions of Hell, up Mount Purgatory, and into the inner precincts of Paradise where he discovers the proper object and source of love. The work includes *Inferno*, *Purgatorio*, and *Paradiso*.

Defoe, Daniel – *The Adventures of Robinson Crusoe*

A shipwrecked young man's struggle to survive on a deserted island forces him to re-evaluate his religious beliefs.

Dickens, Charles – *Great Expectations*

Orphan Pip, a common boy who lives with his aunt and uncle, dreams of being a gentleman. When his ambitions are realized by an undisclosed benefactor, he forgets his roots and takes on airs, hoping to attract the attentions of high-born and disdainful Estella. A startling examination of love, betrayal, and respect, Dickens's coming of age story depicts the true meaning of "gentleman." Also by Dickens: *A Tale of Two Cities*, *A Christmas Carol*, *David Copperfield*, *Nicholas Nickleby*, *Bleak House* and others.

Dillard, Annie – *Pilgrim at Tinker Creek*

This collection of first-person essays narrates a year-long Walden-esque experience in which the persona explores the natural world through imagery in a poetic attempt to better divine the nature of God.

Dumas, Alexandre – *The Three Musketeers*

A swashbuckling suspense tale of three daring defenders of King Louis XIII, and their youthful and idealistic protégé, D'Artagnan, the Three Musketeers combines romance and intrigue to create a fantastically entertaining adventure story of the battle between good and evil in pre-Revolution era France. Also by Dumas: *The Count of Monte Cristo*, *The Man in the Iron Mask.*

Forester, C. S. – *Lieutenant Hornblower*

Eleven volumes of high seas adventure set in the Napoleonic Wars follow the naval career of Horatio Hornblower. See: *The Happy Return*, *Ship of the Line*, *Flying Colours*, *The Commodore, Lord Hornblower*, *Mr. Midshipman Hornblower*, *Lieutenant Hornblower*, *Hornblower and the Atropos*, *Hornblower in the West Indies*, *Hornblower and the Hotspur*, and *Hornblower During the Crisis.*

H. G. Wells – *The Invisible Man*

In this psychological thriller, a young scientist must face the consequences of his experiments. After using himself as the subject of experimental research, the scientist discovers the key to invisibility; yet, he is unable to reverse the effects.

Hawthorne, Nathaniel – *The Scarlet Letter*

Set in Puritan New England, this story traces the effects of hidden and confessed sin in the lives of Hester Prynne and the Reverend Arthur Dimmesdale.

Hemingway, Ernest – *The Old Man and the Sea*

A master of modern American prose, Hemingway's rejection of Christianity is borne out in the nihilistic worldview his works espouse. With no Christian redemption, grace under pressure becomes the character quality most prized. In this short novella, Santiago, an old fisherman plagued by bad luck, catches the largest marlin of his career only to lose it to sharks on his trip to shore. His fight to survive and make sense of the thing forms the substance of the narrative. Also by Hemingway: *The Sun Also Rises*, "The Snows of Kilimanjaro" and other short stories. His short play, "Today Is Friday," is perhaps one of his most revealing works.

Henry, O. – *"The Ransom of Red Chief" and other short stories*

When two ne'er-do-wells kidnap a boy for ransom, they are surprised to find themselves the victims of extortion. A master of his genre, O. Henry distinguishes himself time and again in his collection of short stories, each demonstrating unique humor and a developed sense of irony. Modern Library's *The Best Short Stories of O. Henry* includes 600 of his shorts, including: "The Ransom of Red Chief," "The Gift of the Magi," and "The Last Leaf."

Henty, G. A. – *The Cat of Bubastes*

Set in ancient Egypt, this work of historical fiction follows a conquered prince into servitude in an Egyptian household where, together with his master's son, he seeks to cover up the unintentional slaying of a cat deemed sacred and exposes the deceit and trickery of temple priests, stumbling into a murderous plot against his master's life. Other notable Henty books include: *Beric the Briton*, *In Freedom's Cause*, *The Dragon and the Raven*, *For the Temple*, and *Winning His Spurs*.

Herriot, James – ***All Creatures Great and Small***

English country veterinarian James Herriot writes of his daily interactions with all of God's great creatures. Also by the author, *All Things Bright and Beautiful* and *All Things Wise and Wonderful.*

Heyerdahl, Thor – ***Kon-Tiki***

A 101-day journey across the Pacific on a balsa wood raft to prove an historical theory made history of its own in April of 1947. Battling sharks and leaks and the elements, Heyerdahl and his crew lived one of the greatest ocean adventures of all time.

Hilton, James – ***Good-bye, Mr. Chips***

Dear old Chips, the English schoolmaster, found personal worth and usefulness in spite of his unremarkability. Few are great. Most are common, but mediocrity is not failure. An average life leaves ripples in the lives of many.

Homer – ***The Iliad***

When Menelaus's beloved wife Helen is carried off by Paris the Trojan, all Helen's erstwhile suitors band together to retrieve her. Thus follows the siege of Troy, the exploits of the soldier, Odysseus, and the tragic story of the anti-hero, Achilles, the stories of which comprise the Trojan War Cycle. In the *Iliad*, Achilles, deprived of his war trophy, withdraws from the battle to sulk by his black ships. Nothing assuages his bitter wrath. When his best friend volunteers to take his place at the front and is struck down by the Trojan warrior Hektor, Achilles re-enters the fray, intent on revenge. Homer lays the human condition bare in this beautiful and captivating epic.

Homer – ***The Odyssey***

A sequel to *The Iliad*, this narrative recounts the adventures and exploits of the Achaean hero Odysseus on his ten-year journey home from the Trojan War. Opposed by the god Poseidon and the sea nymph Calypso, Odysseus languishes on a Mediterranean island until the gods pity him and speed him home to Ithaca to rescue his wife and son from the thralls of wicked suitors who impose in his absence.

Hugo, Victor – ***Les Miserables***

Imprisoned for nineteen years for stealing bread to feed his starving family, Jean Valjean returns to an unforgiving society. Yet the kindness and mercy of a local churchman sets him on a noble path to become an epic hero. Hugo imbues his novel with an understanding of the nature of the Law and the redemptive power of self-sacrificial grace.

Irving, Washington – ***The Legend of Sleepy Hollow***

After being rebuffed by the damsel Katrina, schoolmaster Ichabod Crane rides off on his landlord's horse, sees an apparition of a headless horseman, and disappears. Also by Irving: *Rip Van Winkle.*

Jacques, Brian – ***Redwall*** **(series)**

In the tradition of Tolkien's *The Hobbit* and Grahame's *The Wind in the Willows*, Jacques' *Redwall* series teems with talking beasts on important quests. Meet Matthias, a church mouse destined for greatness. Epic in its scope, the battle between good and evil rages within the pages of these stories.

Kipling, Rudyard – ***Captains Courageous***

Harvey Cheyne is the over-indulged son of a millionaire. When he falls overboard from an ocean liner, he is rescued by a Portuguese fishing boat and is forced to work for his passage home.

Latham, Jean Lee – *Carry On, Mr. Bowditch*

The biography of a math genius thrust into indentured servitude by a family that could not support him, Latham's novel depicts the humility, determination, and industry that shape the American identity in the person of Nathaniel Bowditch.

Lee, Harper – *To Kill a Mockingbird*

Lee's tale of a young girl's journey to maturity in Depression-era Alabama is imbued with warmth, humor, and wisdom. Until the recent release of the story's short prequel *Go Set a Watchman*, this treasure remained Lee's one gift to the world.

Lewis, C. S. – *The Space Trilogy: Out of the Silent Planet, Perelandra, and That Hideous Strength*

Lewis's space trilogy follows philologist Elwin Ransom through his space travels and ponders timeless questions of ethics, truth, and spirituality.

Lewis, C. S. – *The Great Divorce*

The narrator, a ghost from the outskirts of hell, takes a day-trip to the outskirts of heaven, the solid land. There he witnesses conversations between the other ghosts and the solid people who travel down the mountain to meet them. In this theodicy, evocative of Dante's *Divine Comedy,* Lewis probes the nature of God, man, and redemption. A mind-stretching masterpiece. Also by Lewis: *The Screwtape Letters*, *Till We Have Faces: A Myth Retold*, and many more works.

London, Jack – *The Call of the Wild*

Naturalist Jack London tells some bleak tales of the dominance of Nature over man; yet, his accounts are exquisitely written and adventure packed. Also by London: *White Fang*, and a plethora of short stories including "To Build A Fire," the most gripping account of that particular activity ever written.

MacLean, Alistair – *The Guns of Navarone*

Set among the islands of the Aegean during WWII, Navarone is the story of a team of allied saboteurs on an impossible mission: infiltrate an impregnable Nazi-held island and destroy the two enormous long-range field guns that prevent the rescue of 2,000 trapped British soldiers.

Marshall, Catherine – *Christy*

Christy, a 19-year-old Christian woman, becomes a missionary schoolmistress in the back hills of Tennessee's Smoky Mountains. There the mountain people challenge her compassion and faith, even as the town's doctor and preacher draw her heart.

Milton, John – *Paradise Lost*

One of Western literature's five great epic poems, *Paradise Lost* dramatizes the story of the Fall of Man in language of unsurpassed beauty and power.

Orwell, George – *Animal Farm*

Orwell paints a vivid picture of a violent political revolution; farm animals unite against the farmer who owns all, works the animal population hard, feeds them little, and sends their offspring to slaughter. Written in 1954, *Animal Farm*'s characters were inspired by the figures of the Russian Revolution. An allegory, the story artistically exposes the results of Stalinist Socialism.

Porter, Gene Stratton – ***A Girl of the Limberlost***

Loveless Elnora lives alone with her bitter and cold mother. Ambitious to make something of her life, she diligently pursues an education, funding it with the specimens she collects in the swamp. Along the way she discovers friendship, love, and a truth about the past which frees her mother to love her.

Potok, Chaim – ***The Chosen***

Reuven and Danny come from rival sects of Judaism; their unlikely friendship becomes a vehicle for Danny's entry into the secular world and a doorway into Reuven's own rabbinical calling. Set in World War II Brooklyn, the story is an eloquent examination of loyalty, friendship and conviction.

Pyle, Howard – ***Men of Iron***

In this adventure-packed tale of fifteenth-century England, young Myles Falworth wins a reputation for courage and independence while still in training at the castle of the great Earl of Mackworth. When he discovers that his blind father had been condemned for treason and is still being hunted by a powerful enemy who is close to the king, he must risk ordeal by battle to win back his family's honor.

Rawlings, Marjorie Kinnan – ***The Yearling***

Perhaps the most beautifully crafted account of a boy's coming-of-age ever written, this is the story of Jody Baxter, a penniless boy from the Florida Everglades, who takes a yearling deer as a pet. His family's fight for survival together with the boy's ardent love for his pet build to create an internal conflict within Jody that transforms him into a man.

Reeves, James – ***Exploits of Don Quixote***

Meet the "beknighted" anti-hero of La Mancha who jousts at windmills and his kind and caring friend, Sancho Panza, in this retelling of Cervantes's classic tale.

Richter, Conrad – ***The Light in the Forest***

Taken captive by Indians as a young boy, young John is raised as a Lenni Lenape. When a government trade returns him to his true home again, feelings of displacement and uncertainties about his own identity rise to the surface.

Shakespeare, William – ***The Riverside Shakespeare***

Shakespeare's works have delighted and inspired readers for generations. While his identity is hotly debated, readers agree that his literary talent remains unsurpassed. Drawn largely from Holinshed's *Chronicles of England, Scotland, and Ireland*, these plays fall loosely into three categories – tragedies, comedies, and histories. Start with *Julius Caesar*, *Macbeth*, *Hamlet*, *Measure for Measure*, *The Taming of the Shrew*, or *Romeo and Juliet*, and don't stop before you have read them all!

Stevenson, Robert Louis – ***Treasure Island***

After meeting an old pirate at his mother's inn, young Jim is whisked into a surreal, high sea expedition, fraught with terrors and piracy, to seek a buried treasure. Along the way, his acquaintance of one Long John Silver challenges his perception of reality and forces him to maturity. Also by Stevenson: *Kidnapped*, *The Black Arrow*.

Ten Boom, Corrie – *The Hiding Place*

In this autobiographical novel set in Holland during WWII, the Ten Boom family hides Jews and political prisoners from Nazi persecution. This act of kindness makes them, too, the target of Nazi aggression. This profound true story of bitterness and redemption, written by the woman who lived through it, explores the love and provision of God in the midst of pain and suffering and the liberating value of forgiveness.

Tolkien, J.R.R. translation – *Sir Gawain and the Green Knight*

When a mysterious Green Knight appears at King Arthur's court on Christmas Eve and challenges someone to give blow for blow with an axe, Sir Gawain nobly agrees. After losing his head, the unearthly knight stands, retrieves it, and reminds Gawain that in a year's time, he, too, must take a blow. At the appointed time, noble Gawain goes in search of the knight to fulfill his obligations.

Tolkien, J.R.R. – *The Lord of the Rings trilogy*

This story of epic proportions traces the wrathful and controlling influence of an evil ring that longs to return to the hand of its wicked lord, and the humble hobbit chosen to destroy it for the good of all of Middle-earth.

Tolstoy, Leo – *Anna Karenina*

Considered by some the greatest novel ever written, *Anna Karenina* is Tolstoy's classic tale of love and adultery set against the backdrop of high society in Moscow and Saint Petersburg. A rich and complex masterpiece, the novel chronicles two parallel stories: It charts the disastrous course of a love affair between Anna, a beautiful married woman, and Count Vronsky, a wealthy army officer. In contrast, it tells the story of the redemptive romantic love between Kitty and Levin. This comparison allows Tolstoy to probe the nature and purpose of romantic love. Tolstoy seamlessly weaves together the lives of dozens of characters, and in doing so captures a breathtaking tapestry of late-nineteenth-century Russian society. As Matthew Arnold wrote in his celebrated essay on Tolstoy, "We are not to take *Anna Karenina* as a work of art; we are to take it as a piece of life." Also by Tolstoy: *War and Peace*, *The Death of Ivan Ilyich.*

Twain, Mark – *The Adventures of Huckleberry Finn*

Vagabond and uncivilized Huckleberry Finn fakes his own death to evade his greedy and abusive father. When he encounters Jim, a runaway slave, in his island hideout, the two team up to float down the Mississippi to freedom. In arguably the greatest American satire, Twain wraps a profound social commentary in an engaging tale full of the homespun humor that was his trademark. Also by Twain: *A Connecticut Yankee in King Arthur's Court*, *The Prince and the Pauper*, and others.

Ullman, James Ramsey – *Banner in the Sky*

Rudi's father died in his attempts to mount the impregnable Citadel, the highest of the Swiss Alps. Propelled by something deep within him, Rudi must finish what his father began to plant his own banner in the sky.

Verne, Jules – *Around the World in 80 Days*

An account of the extraordinary travels of Phileas Fogg and his valet Passepartout, who wager with Fogg's fellow club members to circumnavigate the globe within

80 days. Pursued by Fix, a private detective who believes Fogg to be a bank robber, the pair cross three continents and two oceans on trains, steamers, an elephant, and anything else they can lay their hands on. Will Phileas and Passepartout make it back to London within the 80 days? Also by Verne: *20,000 Leagues Under the Sea*, and *Journey to the Center of the Earth.*

Vernon, Louise – *Ink on His Fingers*

Vernon chronicles the life of Johann Gutenberg, inventor of the printing press with movable type, through the eyes of a young apprentice. Also by Vernon: *The Bible Smuggler, The Beggar's Bible, A Heart Strangely Warmed, The Man Who Laid the Egg*, and *Thunderstorm in the Church.*

Virgil – *The Aeneid*

Some medieval Christians recognized this classic Latin epic to contain a prophetic announcement of the events of the birth of Christ. In fact, its author intended it to trumpet the glory and destiny of Rome. The story itself follows Aeneas, a Trojan who escaped the destruction of his homeland, as he voyages to Italy to found a new city for his displaced people. Shipwrecked in Carthage, he falls in love with the Princess Dido, but his divine mission calls. Full of loyalty, love, betrayal, and murder, this classic draws present readers as readily as it did its contemporaries.

APPENDIX C: GLOSSARY OF LITERARY TERMS

Allegory – a figurative story in which the principal subject is depicted by another subject resembling it in its properties and circumstances; a symbolic representation; a narrative in which abstract ideas are personified; a sustained metaphor, e.g., *Pilgrim's Progress*, *Everyman*

Anaphora – the stylistic repetition of the initial words of a sentence for dramatic effect

Antagonist – the character who impedes the progress of the protagonist towards his goal. Note that this is not necessarily a villain.

Anthropomorphism – Ascribing human qualities to animals or non-human beings

Anti-hero – a protagonist who fails to demonstrate the typical heroic qualities (Charlie Brown, for example)

Archetype – the original pattern after which a thing is made; a model or first form

Authorial Intrusion – a device by which the narrator inserts comments regarding the characters and story in a direct address to the reader

Bard – an oral storyteller

Caesura – a dramatic, poetic pause; most notable in Anglo-Saxon verse in which each line divides neatly in two with two stressed syllables on either side of the break

Cacophony – intentional creation of dissonant sound through syntax

Catharsis – an emotional release provided by an artistic or aesthetic experience

Character – one of the people in a story

Characterization – the creative act of describing and developing a fictional character

Chiasmus – a rhetorical device in which clauses or phrases are repeated in reverse order for effect

Climax – the turning point of a story; the highest point of interest; the peak of tension

Close Reading – reading a second time, paying attention to details; careful reading

Comedy – a dramatic composition which portrays light and humorous characters or utilizes satire, typically with a happy ending

Conflict – the problem that drives the plot of a story forward toward its conclusion

Connotation – the implied meaning of an author's words

Context – text surrounding words that provide significance and communicate meaning; historical and cultural factors surrounding events that give them significance

Criticism – a philosophy that encompasses well-developed viewpoints on the proper way to read, understand, and interpret literature

Dénouement – the disentangling of the intricacies of the plot of a story; also referred to as Falling Action

Dialogue – written conversation between two or more characters

Dramatic Monologue – type of poem in which the poet assumes a persona and delivers a speech (either aloud in soliloquy, or in conversation with an implied listener) the nature of which reveals his ambitions, motives, or personal character

Euphemism –the use of words with positive connotations to disguise a darker meaning

Euphony – the arrangement of words to create harmonious, pleasant sound

Exposition – the introduction of a story, in which the author presents his characters in their setting and places them in an initial conflict that will drive the story forward

Fiction – narrative prose that is not factual. Examples include novel, short story, myth and fable.

Figurative Meaning – meaning that lies beneath the surface; implicit meaning

Figure – a stock character within a story. Examples include the Christ-Figure, the Hero, the Villain, and the Everyman.

Flashback – a device by which an author breaks from a temporal scene to retrospectively fill in narrative details from an earlier event

Foil – a character created to demonstrate the qualities of the hero through comparison and contrast

Foreshadowing – early hints within the text of events that will take place in later in the story

Frame – the external story or context in which the story takes place

Genre – a type of literature, distinguished from other types by form, technique, and subject matter. Genres include fiction, non-fiction, science fiction, fantasy, romance, and poetry.

Hero – a "superman" whose deeds aid the protagonist and resolve the story's conflict

Inversion – a figure of speech by which the writer inverts words for rhetorical effect

Irony – a mode of speech or writing expressing a literal sense contrary to the meaning intended by the speaker (verbal irony), or a situation contrary to what was expected (circumstantial irony), or a theatrical scene in which the audience knows more about a character's words or circumstances than the character himself (dramatic irony)

Juxtaposition – placing two things in close proximity for the sake of comparison; similar to the concept of the literary foil

Kennings – compound word metaphors that suggest abstract ideas, abundant in Anglo-Saxon verse, e.g., *whale road* to signify ocean, *ring giver* to suggest a king

Literal Meaning – the face value of words or idea

Literary Device – a verbal tool employed by an author to enhance the effect of his story. Examples include imagery, alliteration, metaphor and rhyme

Literary Period – the historical era that was the scene of the development of a particular type of literary expression

Litotes – a sarcastic understatement created by a use of a negative expression to convey a positive comment, e.g., "you won't go hungry" for "you will feast"

Malapropism – an intentional syntactical misuse of a word for the sake of humor

Metonymy – a figure of speech by which a thing is named by something commonly associated with it, e.g., boiling water for tea is referenced as putting on the kettle

Meter – the rhythmical composition of a poetic line

Mood – the atmosphere or emotional tone of a work of art

Motif – a theme or idea that appears repeatedly throughout a story and characterizes it

Negative Capability – Keats's idea of the artistic ability to hold two seemingly contradictory truths in tension, not demanding scientific clarity; the ability to live with uncertainty

Non-Fiction – writing that is based in fact. Examples include biographies, news stories, encyclopedia articles, and research papers.

Novel – a long work of fiction

Novella – a short novel or lengthy short story

Paradox – an apparent contradiction

Pathetic Fallacy – the artistic attribution of emotion to inanimate things or animals. This is narrower than personification, as it communicates emotion very specifically.

Persona – Latin for "mask;" the personality assumed by a poet; the voice in which a poet speaks

Personification – a comparison in which human qualities are assigned to inanimate things

Plot – the sequence of events in a story; the simple story line without all of the details

Poem – a verse composition, especially one characterized by economy of linguistic expression, vivid imagery, and intense emotional tone; generally characterized by adherence to rules of structure and form, including rhythm and sometimes rhyme

Point of View – the perspective from which a story is told. Examples include first-person (written from the perspective of the narrator using the first-person pronoun "I"), third-person narrative (written from the perspective of a third party using third-person pronouns like *he, she, they,* and *it*), third-person omniscient narrative (written from the perspective of a third-party witness to the story who has a God's eye view of the events, allowing them to access the internal thought processes of the characters), and third-person limited (written from the perspective of a third party who has a God's eye perspective of the main character, but a view of the other characters which is limited to what may be observed or overheard).

Prose – writing that is not poetry. Examples include essays, novels, history, scientific treatises, journal articles and literary criticism.

Protagonist – the main character in a story; the character whose goals drive the plot

Pun – a play on words, often resulting in humorous effects

Satire – the use of irony, sarcasm, or ridicule to expose, denounce, or deride a particular vice or folly; a literary composition in verse or prose in which such vices or abuses are held up to scorn, derision, or ridicule

Setting – the place and time in which the action of the story occurs

Soliloquy – a monologue delivered by a performer alone onstage, during which he reveals his innermost thoughts to the audience, but not to the other performers

Stock Characters – familiar characters used regularly and interchangeably in a wide variety of stories. Examples include the young lovers, the snake oil salesman, the court jester, and the stiff butler.

Stream of Consciousness – a narrative device by which an author expresses the disordered thoughts running through the mind of a character

Symbolism – the use in literature of a physical object to represent an abstract idea. The object usually carries both a figurative and literal meaning, e.g., a flag represents the ideals of a nation, patriotism, etc.

Synecdoche – a rhetorical device by which a part references a whole, e.g., referring to a car as *wheels*

Tautology – repetition of something syntactically self-evident; redundancy; in logic, a statement necessarily true due to its form

Theme – the underlying universal idea the author hopes to communicate by his story; the author's message; the author's thoughts on his leading subject. Some universal themes include: The Danger of Mob Rule, The Evils of Prejudice, The Pain of Betrayal, The Value of Innocence, Materialism vs. Idealism, The Nature of Pride and Humility, The Folly of Ambition, The Inevitable Triumph of Good Over Evil, The Process of Coming of Age, The Praiseworthiness of Personal Honor, Loyalty, and Survival.

Tragedy – a drama portraying the struggle of a strong-willed protagonist against fate. The downfall of the protagonist usually hinges upon the fatal flaw in his otherwise heroic character.

Voice – the tone of the author; the product of his vocabulary and syntax

APPENDIX D: ADDITIONAL RESOURCES

The following resources may help you apply the *Teaching the Classics* method more effectively in your classroom. Ordering information can be found at www.centerforlit.com.

Ready Readers

Bound collections of teacher guides for hand-picked classic books at every grade level. Each teacher guide provides a selection of questions from the Socratic List (with complete answers!) for specific stories, offering teachers a ready-made set of discussion notes.

Reading Roadmaps

A K–12 Scope and Sequence manual that turns the *Teaching the Classics* method into a formal curriculum for reading and literature. *Reading Roadmaps* includes complete annotated reading lists for every grade level with over two hundred recommended titles. Each list entry includes a summary of the conflict, plot, themes and literary devices found in the story, as well as an alternate title.

Worldview Detective

A two-hour teacher training seminar similar in style and format to *Teaching the Classics*, but designed to extend the discussion of literature into worldview analysis. Having learned to ask and answer the question, "what does the story say?" teachers and students can now learn to ask, "what does the author believe?"

The Classics Club

A series of videos presenting classroom discussions of specific stories using the *Teaching the Classics* method. Taught by experienced *Teaching the Classics* instructors, these videos demonstrate our discussion techniques and provide complete treatment of classic works of literature.

Online Academy

Live online literature and writing classes for students in grades 5–12 featuring the *Teaching the Classics* approach to literature, taught by experienced Center For Lit teachers.

The Pelican Society

An online community of teachers, parents, and readers interested in the Center For Lit approach to all things literary. Members receive exclusive access to a variety of resources, including product discounts, classroom resources, audio books, live events, and more.